W9-CAO-474

JUDAISM IN SIGMUND FREUD'S WORLD

By

EARL A. GROLLMAN

FOREWORD BY NATHAN W. ACKERMAN, M.D.

APPLETON-CENTURY NEW YORK
BY SPECIAL ARRANGEMENT WITH
BLOCH PUBLISHING COMPANY

Library of Congress Catalogue Card Number 65-19610

To My Parents

In Grateful Appreciation

Of Their Love And Example

ACKNOWLEDGMENTS

Indebtedness is acknowledged to far more persons than can be mentioned by name. How can one even begin to thank all those whose friendship and assistance have made this work possible?

To Nathan W. Ackerman, Erich Lindemann, Gordon W. Allport, Stanley H. Cath, Robert L. Katz, I am grateful for their information, guidance and assistance.

To my wife, Netta, I express my affection for her gentle understanding and encouragement even through periods of neglect.

To Helen Margalith I owe much for her guidance, confidence and inspiration.

To Lillian Tigar, my debt is immeasurable. Her criticisms and helpful suggestions have removed many a rough spot in the style and the content of this work. Her dedication was an extracurricular task performed late at night after an active day as the Executive Secretary of Beth El Temple.

To Carol Stone, I acknowledge with thanks her helpfulness in many important ways, and especially for a secretarial task done with skill and painstaking care and to Fay Galgay for her assistance in typing the original research.

To Allen Spiegel, for lending his craftsmanship and consummate skill, I am deeply grateful.

And last but not least, my thanks are extended to the men and women and children of the Beth El Temple Center, Belmont, Massachusetts for fourteen years of challenge and blessing.

E. A. G.

TABLE OF CONTENTS

FOREWORD

This book poses an intriguing question. What can we glean, in close retrospective study, of the influence of Freud's Jewishness on the man, the scientist, the creator? What may we possibly understand of the mysterious connections between his ethnic identity, his ideas, and the world's reception of them? The significance of the question runs deep. It extends far beyond the limits of Freud's own life and work; it is the fundamental problem of sameness and difference in human relations.

In posing the question, the author wisely makes no pretense of a final answer. What is meaningful, as this work unmistakably reveals, is not so much the answer, but rather the fascination and excitement of the search itself. The author embarks on his voyage of discovery much in the spirit of Freud's own intrepid explorations of the depths of the human mind. This book is an adventure for the curious. Its aim is "expository—to summarize the teachings of Freud in the Jewish setting of his time." In essence, this is a biographical, social-historical study of Freud, in which context the author delicately illuminates the significance of Jew-Gentile interaction. In fulfilling this mission, he shows a commendable, open-minded spirit, pursuing the ramifications of the problem with great care, scrupulous documentation and considered objectivity.

That Freud was a Jew made a difference, a difference to Jews and Christians alike; in fact to all of humanity. But what difference is the question! For all of his life, Freud suffered the stings and arrows of anti-Semitism; for all of his life, he clung with a stern dignity to his Jewishness. "My parents were Jews and I have remained a Jew myself." And yet, in this extraordinary life story, there lies hidden the strangest paradox. Freud declared himself unequivocally to be a "non-believer." He diagnosed all formal religions as neurosis. Despite this, were he not a Jew, psychoanalysis might never have been born. To Oskar Pfister, his Protestant Clergyman friend and follower, he wrote with inimitable pungency, "How comes it that not one of the Godly ever devised psychoanalysis, and that one had to wait for a Godless Jew?" A Godless Jew, I wonder!

Psychoanalysis, which revolutionized our view of human nature, designed a new philosophy of mental healing, pervasively influenced psychiatry, medicine, social science, literature and the arts, was dubbed by the Nazis, "the pornographic Jewish specialty"! What a travesty!

And yet, the question persists. Is psychoanalysis a Jewish invention? The answer is neither yes nor no; it is yes and no. Freud was first, last, always a Jew, but a very special kind of Jew. To remain only a Jew was for Freud a source of perpetual anguish. He yearned for a "ticket of admission" to the wider culture, but not at the cost of sacrificing his Jewishness. Instead, he asserted a dual claim to belong to the family of man, as a Jew and as a human being. He worried lest the world refuse to listen to a Jew; it did.

In this thoughtful study, one discovers much that is rich and exciting. To give the reader a foretaste of what he may find here, I shall extract from the text a few choice tid-bits.

Freud was raised in a "filthy, over-crowded ghetto." . . . "His life coincided with a disastrous chapter in Jewish history." His father was an aloof man, considerably older than his mother. Freud felt somewhat removed from his father but was his mother's favorite. In her heart, he was destined for greatness. In the tender years of his childhood, he was cared for by a Catholic nurse who preached heaven and hell and took him with her to church. With his flare for the dramatic, he called her "that prehistoric old woman." As a boy, he dreamed of a military career, of being a general; he would be a martyred hero. In real life, he was "shunned and despised" for being a Jew. He felt mortified by his father's meek submission to Jew-baiters. For Freud, it was not possible to surrender to the dictum, "a Jew never fights back."

He stood his ground against the abuse of anti-Semites. He cowed them with his angry glare. Like a Jew, he fought back, not with his hands, but with ideas. He suffered for his Jewishness. "In my opinion, we have as Jews to develop a little masochism." In the anti-Semitic climate of his time, he was pressured out of a strictly academic career, pushed into private clinical practice and for seventeen years denied a professorship.

The meaning of Freud's Jewishness is poignantly disclosed here. The Jew is a marginal being. He is "prescribed from the compact majority." Excluded from the circles of Christians, he must band together with other Jews. However maligned, he grows by his suffering. It strengthens his spirit; it adds to his energy. The Jew is more sensitive, more self-critical, less sure. He knows his short-comings. "A Jew must create a compensating culture or take the gamble of going stark crazy." . . . "What bound me to Judaism . . . was not belief, and not national pride. . . . There were other considerations which made the attractiveness of Judaism and Jews irresistible . . . many obscure forces and emotions, all the more powerful the less they were defined in words." . . . "Only to my Jewish nature did I owe the two qualities which had become indispensable to me on my hard road. Because I was a Jew, I found myself free of many prejudices and being a Jew, I was prepared to enter opposition and to renounce agreement with the compact majority."

Here in Freud's own inspired words, we are privileged to feel the full impact of what it means to be a Jew in a world governed by the "compact majority."

The Jew prizes learning and wisdom. For him, learning is the precondition of a sound mind. As an outsider, he is impelled to look above and beyond the walls of his culture. Nietzsche once said, "No man can see over his head." Yet this is exactly what Freud accomplished.

The Jew cherishes liberty. Trained in servitude, he treasures freedom above all else. "We Jews have always known how to respect spiritual values. We preserved our ideas, and, because of them, we have survived to this day."

The Jew is devoted to his family. His first concern is the future of his children. He seeks to educate them "in such a way that they can more freely cross the frontiers."

The Jew is a pessimist. He feels oppressed by "the unworthiness of human beings, the hollowness of the ideas of civilization."

The Jew is a non-conformist, in fact, a "wicked heretic." But he is heretical in the service of the good. He gives voice to the conscience of civilization.

However abused, the Jew must remain true to his people; there is no other way. "It always seemed to me not only shameful but downright senseless to deny it."

Yet there was also the other side of the picture. Freud chafed at the strictures imposed upon him as a Jew. Never for an instant did he surrender the tortuous struggle to break through the dark walls of the ghetto into the light and larger world. In his anxiety for all people to listen to his ideas, he welcomed into the psychoanalytic fold the non-Jew, Carl Jung. Much against the misgivings of his Jewish colleagues, he insisted that Jung be elected President of the International Psychoanalytic Association. His comment in this circumstance is revealing, "Most of you are Jews and incompetent to win friends for the new movement. . . . I am weary of being perpetually attacked. . . . This Swiss (Jung) will save us." What happened later makes of this episode a stark irony. To this day, it remains a blight on Jung's brilliant career that he finally seemed to take sides with the Nazis in attacking the "Jewish psychology," as seeing "only faults and not virtues." In the eyes of his Christian confreres, Jung stands indicted as "crypto-anti-Semitic."

That Freud waged a life-long battle against the scourges of mankind, madness, prejudice and human cruelty, is no accident. His piercing insights into the dark, tortuous depths of the suffering psyche are now part of our everyday vocabulary. But his war against prejudice and against man's inhumanity to man are less widely appreciated.

Between prejudice, violence and mental illness, there are, in fact, deep connections. It is precisely the human striving to belong that influences our proneness both to prejudice and mental illness. Both have to do with human relations. Prejudice is a "dislike of the unlike." It signifies a hostile emotion against people who are different, simply because they are different. Mental health has to do with the kind of person one is and the way one behaves with other people because one is that kind of person. A person who is emotionally sick behaves in a rigid, constricted, repetitive way. He ceases gradually to learn from experience, to test reality and to grow. A prejudiced person shows similar qualities. He is ridden with fear and mistrust. He feels weak, exposed, vulnerable to attack and injury. He fears change, he fears the unknown and loses the capacity to learn. He exploits his prejudice to evade consciousness of fear, to buttress self-esteem and to gain a false sense of power.

The person tending to mental breakdown leans on

his prejudice. To stave off his own threatened collapse, he tries, by means of scapegoating, to break down someone else. But prejudice is a feeble barricade. It is a weak Maginot Line. Insofar as the effort to hold one's self together by tearing another down is irrational, the prejudicial barricade ultimately collapses like a house of cards. Witch-hunting is hardly a safeguard for anyone's sanity. Through its very irrational essence, prejudice becomes a destructive force in society. It is contagious; it is inherently violent and cruel. It is used in an utterly futile way to fortify a master-slave pattern of human relations, as if the victim exists only to aggrandize the attacker—a perverted design for living in which power is exalted for its own sake. Prejudice, thought control, character assassination, master-slave relations are all of a piece. They are steps along the path of no return to mass madness and mass suicide.

If we would seek the antidote to save our civilization, we must remember that prejudices attached to ethnic, religious, and color differences are intimately associated with other forms of prejudice. In Nazi Germany, the clock was turned back. Women were once again demeaned, treated as chattel and as breeding machines. Not only was woman divided from man, but also son from father; thus it becomes male against female, child against parent, youth against the elders. This is prejudice with a vengeance, suicidal prejudice. What is at stake are all the values of civilized living.

It is of the essence to identify the parallelism of private and public forms of prejudice. Private types of prejudice emerge in the intimacies of family life; they are more subtle, more elusive, but no less cancerous. I refer here to the prejudice for one sex against another, for the younger generation against the older one, for money and power against cultural values, for duty and discipline against freedom, spontaneity and pleasure, for brawn against brain, for rightist versus a leftist ideology, and so forth. The personal and private forms of prejudice invade the public domain. They provide the emotional energy, the driving force for the unconscious adoption of the common prejudices in the community against the Jew, the Negro, the Puerto Rican and the Chinese.

Prejudice is the fear of the unknown, the suspicion of the stranger in our midst. It is surely not caused by the accident of not knowing the other person; it is rather the tenacious refusal to know and to trust the other that breeds prejudice. Human differences are here to stay. Inevitably, they engender some conflict. But conflict over differences may be benign as well as malignant. It can either catalyze or paralyze the growth of human relations. Differences among people are the symbol of man's incompleteness. Man is incomplete without woman, woman is incomplete without child; Christian is incomplete without Jew; the white is incomplete without Negro.

It is the nature of man that he feels plagued by his difference, by his sense of incompleteness. To feel incomplete is to feel exposed and vulnerable, to struggle with the anxiety of aloneness and dying. From birth to death, man struggles fiercely to deny this threat, to master it by seeking to feel complete, all-powerful and perfect. This he can never do. To be super-human is to be non-human. In a paradoxical sense, this is the real and final death. The issue is not one of achieving completeness, therefore, but rather the never-ending quest that is meaningful; it lends to life its quality of excitement, adventure and challenge. We cherish the ideal but must come to terms with the real. We must learn to live with the anxiety of incompleteness, aloneness and dying. By facing death, we are enabled to live life. The pain of incompleteness is assuaged if we make rational, creative use of conflict over difference. Man has two alternatives in dealing with difference; he can choose the sick or the healthy way.

In the intimacies of family life, and in the family of nations, unfortunately, we sometimes choose the sick way. We allow ourselves to be trapped by the differences of the haves and the have nots. Driven by fright, we become obsessed that there is not enough to go around—not enough food, love, security, status and power. Intolerance of the anxiety of difference and incompleteness becomes the contagion of our time. The true deficiency is not in the lack of quantity, but rather in the distribution of what we possess. We do, in fact, have enough for everybody. The real trouble lies in a disorder of the circulatory system of society. Nonetheless, the delusion of "not enough" persists. It evokes a prejudicial pressure for sacrifice. One part of the family of man must be sacrificed to serve and aggrandize the other. One part builds itself up by tearing the other down. The profit of the one becomes loss on the other. This is a false ethic in human relations. The dread of deprivation, the obsession of "not enough" impels recourse to anachronistic values, and sick, regressive defenses against anxiety, the urge to greed, possessiveness, and power, to seize the commanding position of master while reducing the other to the position of slave.

Human history reveals unmistakably that the path of prejudice and the violence of master-slave relations are not the way to safety. Such a path is cannibalistic, barbaric and sick; it cannot work.

In the present era of acute social unrest, explosions of mass prejudice and mass madness are a clear and present danger. They are a contagious force that can spread havoc like a prairie fire. The decimation of millions of Jews by the Nazis may be as nothing compared to the possible devastation of a war between the light and dark-skinned peoples of the world. Atomic power is, after all, only a means. The real threat lies in the risk of the misuse of this weapon by a sick, decadent society.

It is against the backdrop of this fundamental problem of sameness and difference in human relations that we must weigh the worth of this book. We are indebted to the author for shedding further light on this question. This record of Freud's personal struggle with Jew-Gentile tensions is a scholarly book, well written and richly rewarding.

NATHAN W. ACKERMAN, M. D.
Associate Clinical Professor of Psychiatry, Columbia University; Supervising and Research Psychiatrist, Family Mental Health Clinic, Jewish Family Service, New York City.

INTRODUCTION

Sigmund Freud, the scientist who also happened to be a Jew, consciously treated religion as an illusion even though he paid a great deal of attention to it. This book attempts to clarify the connection between Freud's personal life and psychology, and his psychology of religion.

There are those who claim that Freud was not really anti-religious and cite one of his first and most famous case histories, known as "Wolfman," which involved a religious experience. At the age of three, the patient had developed a behavior disturbance characterized by the fear of wolves. The child's mother attempted on her own to render the therapeutic effect of religious instruction. "His mother determined to make him acquainted with the Bible story in the hope of distracting and elevating him. Moreover, she succeeded; his initiation into religion brought the phase to an end." The animal phobia disappeared and Freud concluded that "the battle ended in a victory for faith . . . Religion achieved all the aims . . . It put a restraint on his sexual impulsions by affording them a sublimation and a safe mooring."

Speaking of the ethical values of religion, Freud said: "He who knows nothing of these values is ignorant indeed, and he who has assimilated them may consider himself enriched.'' Protagonists go one step further and quote his comment in *The Future of an Illusion* concerning that valuable aspect of religion which strengthens the power of society to enforce ethical behavior.

Added to this positive belief in the worth of religion was Freud's thought that psychoanalysis could be a boon to pastoral counseling. He wrote in a letter to his disciple, Rev. Oskar Pfister: ''In itself, psychoanalysis is neither religious nor the opposite, but an important instrument which can serve the clergy as well as the laity, when it is used to free suffering people. I have been very struck at realizing how I had never thought of the extraordinary help the psychoanalytic method can be in pastoral work, probably because wicked heretics like myself are far away from that circle.''

Despite the fact that Freud, in a humorous vein of self-evaluation and understatement, called himself ''an unrepentant atheist,'' some religionists sincerely believe that Freud's ''atheistic'' theory can admirably and effectively be applied to religious thought. The Vicar of the University Church in Oxford, Rev. R. S. Lee wrote in his *Freud and Christianity:* ''Psychoanalysis can cleanse Christianity of its non-Christian elements, and in general the result of applying psychoanalysis to the understanding of religious beliefs is likely to cause some profound modifications in religious thought and practice.'' This is affirmed in Jewish thought in Rabbi Joshua Loth Liebman's *Peace of Mind.* He discussed ''. . . the psychological discoveries about conduct and motive that are really the most recent syllables of the divine''; that ". . . men who are inwardly tormented and emotionally unhappy can never be good partners of God''; and that ". . . a wise religion is indispensable to peace of mind.'' The book concludes with a list of "commandments of a new morality,'' the first of which is: "Thou shalt not be afraid of thy hidden impulses.''

There are also psychiatrists passionately committed to the marriage of religion and psychology. Among these is Karl Stern, who felt that Freud, too, would approve of the match between the two disciplines. Stern, in his *Third Revolution,* attempted to demonstrate that Freud did not really mean what he said in derogation of religion, and that perhaps the founder of psychoanalysis was more religious than many of his most devout critics.

Vigorous dissenters to these views are legion. There are authorities who distrust the reconciliation of Freudian thought with religion. O. Hobart Mowrer not only attacked Freud's medical approach as nontherapeutic and pernicious but explained the mysterious blending of psychiatry and religion (Protestant fundamentalism) in this way: "Calvin saddled us with the doctrine of predestination and divine election; and Freud spoke of psychic determinism and the tyranny of the unconscious . . . Psychoanalysis goes Protestant theology one better and makes us not only unable to help ourselves in the matter of 'recovery' but also blameless and unaccountable for having gotten ourselves into our neurotic predicament in the first place.'' Unfortunately, many commentators made Freud and psychoanalysis synonymous, apparently overlooking the dynamic contributions subsequently made to the field of Ego Psychology.

By endeavoring to blend Freud's own statements into the historical milieu of his time, a clearer picture of the birth pangs of Freud's ideas on religion unfolds. For the social scientist, this may prove helpful in discerning how the human self emerges within a community and coexists with society. Clergymen may find this book of assistance in understanding Freud's views on religion when examined against the setting of his life and times.

The study of any subject is always enhanced by the comments of eminent scholars in related fields. Thus, in examining the development of Freud's attitudes on religion, we call upon the historian who deals with the fidelity of the chronicles, both ancient and modern. The psychologist adds his concern with the traits, feelings, actions and attributes of the mind. We turn to the sociologist whose domain is the forms, institutions and functions of groups. With these diverse branches of knowledge, each invested with unique and respective nomenclatures, now combining in loose formulation to guide us in our considerations, we seek light and clarification of the complex subject of *Judaism in Sigmund Freud's World.*

"Anatomy of Anti-Semitism" (Part I), sets the historical stage of the world before Freud, with the sociological and psychological description of anti-Semitism. Sociologists affirm the significance of the social milieu in which the infant is born. Customs and institutions have meaning and purpose in meeting the individual's distinctive needs. Both personality and culture evolve from the interplay between human needs and the external world. Of course man also has instinctual drives. These must be understood in light of the unique physical, economic and political conditions of a group's dynamic daily life. As Veblen, Pareto, and Thurman Arnold demonstrated, an individual's thinking is clothed by his biological equipment as well as his adjustment to his world as understood through his family and social hierarchies. Environment, social and physical, is more than a haphazard assortment of artifacts joined together in a fortuitous manner. Rather, the social milieu constitutes a functioning, active, working totality, as truly alive as the individuals who are a breathing, thinking and living part of the entire system.

Also detailed are various interpretations of the psychological mechanisms unconsciously integrated into the everyday life of the religious person. Freud's analysis of the basic reason for Jews adopting defense mechanisms even included his thoughts about "Jewish humor." Anti-Semitism was directly related to the evolution of the Jews' religious rituals and to their attitudes which were passed on to succeeding generations.

Concepts of the mechanism of defense appeared as early as 1894 in Freud's paper entitled *The Defence of Neuro-Psychoses.* By the time of his *Interpretation of Dreams* (1900) he had named the mechanisms of repression, projection, compensation, displacement and identification. Five years later in the *Three Contributions to the Theory of Sex,* reaction-formation, fixation and regression were added. Bernard Hart popularized these concepts in a book published in 1912 entitled *Psychology of Insanity.* These mechanisms, although today domesticated and revised, have an important place in our social scientific textbooks.

"The Essence of Jewishness" (Part II), establishes Freud's beliefs about his Jewish heritage. He often noted the obstacles created by the accident of his Jewish birth and yet maintained that he would never relinquish claims to his religion. Although Freud was considered a non-believer and even stated his disavowals of the rituals and rites, he did feel that he retained the best attributes of the faith. Numerous biographers noted that his home life was warm and loving, that learning occupied an extremely high priority and that he had a strong feeling of identification with other Jews. Even his doctrine concerning the powerful drive of sexual urges grew out of Freud's interpretation of the basic ingredients of Jewishness.

"Sigmund Freud, His Religion and His World" (Part III), is an historic sourcebook of Freud's life and teachings. Freud speaks for himself against the background of his time. In a long life which spanned almost half of the nineteenth century and more than a third of the twentieth until his death in 1939 at the age of 83, Freud left an indelible imprint upon literature, education, sociology, anthropology, art and religion. His influence on the world of thought and letters was imposing. Like his kinsman, Baruch Spinoza, he examined life *sub specie aeternatis* (in its universal form or under the aspect of Eternity) and aided in the transvaluation of thought into many collateral fields.

Scattered throughout his writings, from the early 1890's to the late 1930's, his ideas were continually revised, modified, discarded, reworded and expanded. Ernest Jones, Freud's biographer, documented the fact that Freud's work must be approached not as a unified body of thought, but as a series of stages of development in which successive changes are involved. By chronicling individual years, this book follows the advice of Ira Progoff in *Depth Psychology and Modern Man:* "My investigation of the personalities and writings of Freud . . . has indicated that an historical approach is essential if we wish to place ourselves in a position where we can understand the significance of past studies in terms of present needs."

Although many quotations have been selected to illustrate points, they should not be treated as definitive truths but rather as opinions to be weighed and evaluated. The selections attempt to clarify Freud's life and psychology of religion as well as his teachings in the light of the contemporary Jewish setting. Anti-Semitism, one of the most constant factors during the period of Freud's life span, deeply affected the beliefs of the founder of psychoanalysis. The complexities of anti-Semitism are expressed with deep understanding in the following citation by Ackerman and Jahoda: "For the anti-Semite, the Jew is a living Rorschach inkblot. His alleged and sometimes actual qualities are so manifold and so inconsistent, so ambiguous and indeterminate, that the anti-Semite sees whatever he needs to see in the Jew."

EARL A. GROLLMAN, D. D.

JUDAISM IN SIGMUND FREUD'S WORLD

I. AN ANATOMY OF ANTI-SEMITISM

In 313, Christianity became the official religion of Rome. Though anti-Jewish feelings had existed before the ascendancy of the Church, this preceding sporadic hostility could not be compared with the organized hatred that now appeared. New laws were enacted which further restricted freedom for the Jew. Repressive measures were officially affirmed once the Church acquired imperial control. Sermons by John Chrysostom in 387 demonstrated how hatred and detestation of the Jews could be expressed with deadly effect.

Part of the strength of the antipathy was the fact that Christianity was of Jewish origin. Jesus was a Jew. Christians also believed in the Old Testament. The Jews, by denying their own kin, Jesus, stood out as the one non-conformist minority religious group. Judaism was the only non-Christian religion found to any extent in Europe.

Theological reasoning supplied the evidence for the enmity. From a Christological viewpoint, the historical mission of the Jews came to an end when Christianity came into being. After the Biblical drama was consummated in the rise of the Church, the Jew forfeited his covenantal status and his very relationship to the Biblical past. Hebrew Scriptures, which the Church appropriated, were interpreted to designate

Christians as the only believers mentioned in the Old Testament. All the rebukes for backsliding and threats of punishment were then applied to the People of the Book, the Jews. The interpretation of both the Old and the New Testament planted in many Christian minds an ignoble image of Judaism. It was reasoned that since the Jews were asserted to be God's Chosen People, they must be hounded until they accepted the true Messiah—their very own Jesus.

Antagonisms arose against the Christ-givers. Hostility was unconsciously a means of protest for those who felt that the yoke of Christianity was a repression of their own unholy needs and desires. An unconscious reasoning could be as follows: If it were not for Judaism, there would be no Christianity. If he were not a Christian, then he would not be bound to a moral code of truth, honor, fidelity, monogamy. Since the repressed desire for infidelity was too painful to contemplate, anti-Semitism became a way of attacking Judaism as teacher, and Christianity as receiver, of the moral teachings. In later years, a Nazi youth group song declared: "Pope and Rabbi shall be gone. We want to be pagans once again."

The worst defamation perpetrated by the Church labeled the Jews as "Christ-Killers." Sigmund Freud explained this phenomenon on the basis of the death wishes against the parent of the same sex. The experience of the Oedipus Conflict is that the boy is sexually attracted to the mother and therefore envies and despises the father as the possessor of the loved woman. The father as the watchful censor takes the joy out of life by frustrating the wishes of the infant and by imposing an arbitrary authority upon the child. A strong inclination to the murdering of one's father (patricide) exists. This leads to the desire to kill not only the human father but the Heavenly Father-God. (According to Freud, while the Bible reads that God made man in His image, it should be said that man made God in the image of the superego, or that man created God in his father's image.) Freud postulated a hypothesis about the origin of the Oedipus Complex to a prehistoric period when mankind was organized in hordes, led by a father-chief who was killed and eaten by his sons. Anti-Semitism was thus a revolt against the father and the Father-God, of which the Jew is the symbol. According to this view, the Jews bore not only the guilt for the rejection of Jesus as the Christ, the Messiah, but were responsible for his crucifixion as well. These two charges formed an indictment for all subsequent ages.

Textbooks used by parochial schools incorporated these thoughts: "Pilate gave the Jews the choice between Jesus and Barabbas . . . The Jews chose Barabbas, and asked for Jesus to be put to death . . . The Jews were pitiless and clamored 'Crucify Him.' " Because of this alleged heinous act, some Christians developed the theory that Jews must exist to prove that only by their ultimate conversion could the Church emerge triumphant and usher in the kingdom of God. In the meantime, conditions were created so that the Jew could not enjoy life, for eventual happiness was contingent upon the acceptance of the true Messiah. Therefore, the Jews were regarded as a people outside the pale of Christian fellowship, who were to be accursed forever and continually exposed to the perpetual wrath of God. A conviction in Western Europe insisted that Jews be cut off from their fellowman, thus making ordinary relations with them difficult to effect and when effected, sinful. With anti-Semitism the established teaching, the doctrine became fixed in a tradition that was passed on to each new generation in a socialization process.

In defense, the Jew was forced to intensify his own cohesiveness into an ethnocentric cultural-religious group. Just as a nation is never so unified as in wartime, so the Jew, systematically excluded from occupations, housing, and social outlets, was to find his security through strengthening the in-group ties. The distinctiveness of Judaism was forcibly retained in the midst of a dynamically expanding Christianity. By dispersions and exiles, Jews became conspicuous as a different religious group and therefore a "dangerous" people. In their isolation, they were misunderstood, pillaged, and oppressed. Their blood was spilled in atonement for the death of the crucified, whose cries for mercy were now drowned in the tumult of the disciples' fanaticism and hatred.

Austria, the homeland of Sigmund Freud, displayed dramatically this intolerance and prejudice from the first reliable account of the presence of Jews in the country. An ordinance during the reign of Louis the Child (899–911) related to discriminatory practices against Jewish merchants. Many Jewish traders of the Rhine country had emigrated to the East Mark of the Holy Roman Empire, later known as Austria. This was the era when cities began and commerce developed. Jews were denied legal rights and permitted to reside in the community only at the pleasure of the princes. Since the royal treasuries were so often empty, Jews were utilized effectively as revenue officers to extract money from the unwilling Christian citizenry. With their "high visibility" the Jews further antagonized the rank and file by being the "royal usurers." The Jew was attracted into marginal banking activities for one reason. He was forbidden to engage in other occupations.

The next reference to a Jew in Austria was in 1194 when Leopold V appointed a Shlomo to the head of the mint, the *super officium monetae*. Jews who were traders or bankers still were welcomed by Emperor Frederick II and in 1204, the Jewish community erected their first synagogue in Vienna. For a brief period the Princes of Babenberg entrusted the exclusive care of finances to Jewish officials and granted them titles of honor. Life was becoming more optimistic. A royal decree protected Jewish inhabitants against murder, assault, and even forced baptism.

However, more and more Christians were now entering the formerly marginal occupations associated with "Jewish trade." As citizens and members of the dominant religion they wanted to eliminate the factor of competition. Historically there have been recorded cases of aggression against minorities entirely as a consequence of their economic success, even when they were willing to "keep their place." As for the Jews in Austria, the economic motive for their suppression was clear. A protest was soon lodged by the Christians of Vienna to Frederick to desist from aiding and abetting the Jews.

The cleavage between Jew and Christian was sharpened not only by invisible thoughts and beliefs but by a visible reality. In 1215 Pope Innocent III enacted the Lateran Council Edict decreeing that every Jew above the age of childhood wear a distinctive mark such as a circle of yellow cloth to designate his inferior status. This yellow badge was also the ignominious emblem of the prostitute. In addition, the 1,500 dignitaries who had come to Rome to consider the problem of disciplining heretics further legislated that Jews could not charge high rates of interest for loaning money, nor could they hold public office or employ Christian domestics. Rudolph I, the First Habsburg, founder of the Imperial House of Austria and member of the Ecclesiastical Christian Synod, carried forth the wishes of the Holy See by ordaining that the Jew distinguish himself by wearing a differentiating and disfiguring pointed hat—the *pileum cornutum.* As a consequence of the Vienna Church synod in 1267, masses of people were encouraged by the Emperor to incite bloodshed and massacres. The Jew was pelted and stoned, spat upon and cursed. Many of the synagogue laments which are preserved in the liturgy commemorate the elegy of this period.

Meanwhile more and more Christians turned to trade and by the fourteenth century outnumbered the Jews in this area of economic enterprise. Unwilling to compete with their Jewish rivals, who were both more experienced and sometimes had the advantage of connections with their fellow-Jews in distant commercial cities, Christian businessmen urged the total exclusion of Jews from all trading. Of course, the underlying reason of the dominant group was to appropriate the best positions for themselves. Although the economic motive was not the only consideration, it was probably one of the most important factors determining the origin and extension of their prejudice. In 1316, Austrian Jews were forbidden to make clothes on pain of forfeiting the garments. The gradual broadening of Christendom to the control of every act of life excluded the Jew not only from the tenure of land, but from artisan and commerical guilds. Jews could participate only in those occupations which were ventures of private risk-taking. The economic welfare became closely related to large cities, which meant that the Jew had to center himself in urban areas. Since the Christian peasant on the farm looked with envy upon the materialistic city values and at the same time despised the vulgar estimations identified with metropolitan living, the ambivalence was personified in an enlarged hostility against the Jew—the symbol of urbanity. The Jew was hated primarily because he served as an emblem of city life. To the Austrian tiller of the soil, the Jew became the token of the monster, the all-dominant, much-feared city.

The Hussite Wars (1419–1436) brought new troubles to the Jews of Austria. John Huss, the Bohemian reformer, denounced the practice of indulgence, masses for the dead, and private confessions. He was in turn burned at the stake. The Dominicans, fighting the Hussites, blamed the Jews for these events. Catholics accused the Jews of secretly supplying the enemy with money and arms. The Jews became the convenient scapegoat at a time when the authority of the Church or State was threatened. Demagogues climbed to power by preaching a doctrine of nationalism—usually a unity induced through artificially stimulated fears of a universal Jewish plot. Support was frequently gained when the power complex would hearken back to Jewish business competition and then promise prosperity by the liquidation of Jewish economic and professional activity. In later years, the famous forgery known as the *Protocols of Zion* was published anew whenever a scapegoat was needed. The document appeared in Russia to prove that the Jews were responsible for the disaster of the war with Japan; in England, at a time of severe industrial distress; in Damascus, in connection with Arab-Jewish riots; and it was outlined in twenty pages of *Mein Kampf* to aid the campaign of the National Socialists. Meanwhile, in Vienna, as a result of the Hussites, the Jews, the historic scapegoats, were cut down, their property confiscated by the Dukes and their houses given over to the Christians. The synagogue of Vienna was destroyed and its stones turned over to the university for the construction of a new building. Catholic priests came to the surviving Jews in hope of mass conversions to the "Prince of Peace." Many Jews preferred to slay themselves and their families. Those who were imprisoned were burned at the stake. In Vienna, more than a hundred perished in a single field near the Danube. For a long time, no Jew was to be found in Austria.

But the Jew was to return. The rulers needed him. A

community of individuals capable of producing a considerable yield of actual coin was not easily replaced. Jews were an asset to the royal coffers. So-called court Jews were tolerated only as long as they paid a tax far in excess of the price demanded of other citizens. Occasionally, a benevolent despot such as Rudolph II would issue an edict to one of the Bishops that a court Jew was not to be deprived of his rights. Rudolph expressed his appreciation to the President of the Jewish community, who was also the Official Receiver of Taxes, Jacob Bassevi. There was conferred upon him in 1570, the first title of nobility ever bestowed upon an Austrian Jew: "von Treuenberg." Not only was Jacob Bassevi von Treuenberg given the privilege of residing in sections otherwise prohibited to Jews, he was also instrumental in protecting the entire Jewish community from mercenary soldiers during the Thirty Years War.

Peace and prosperity were short lived. In order not to be decried by his contemporaries as an ally of these aliens, Rudolph II instituted an even more excessive burden of taxation. When the Jews could not serve him in the accustomed lucrative fashion, the Emperor ordered them to be expelled from the archduchy of Austria. The ordeal was augmented by further restrictions from the Church councils. Martin Luther (1483–1546) began his career as a liberal crusader for the Jew and denounced the hypocrisy of the Church. He said: "Our fools, the popes, bishops, sophists, and monks, have hitherto conducted themselves toward the Jews in such a manner that he who was a good Christian would have preferred to be a Jew. And if I had been a Jew and had seen such blockheads and louts ruling and teaching Christianity, I would have become a swine rather than a Christian, because they have treated the Jews like dogs, and not like human beings." Later, Luther was to change. He urged the princes to destroy the synagogues and confiscate the wealth of the Jew.

How did the Jews survive such unremitting woe? Suffering received a special emphasis. They quoted Levi Yitzhok: "It is not why I suffer but only whether I suffer for Thy sake." Their pains were viewed as a matter of pride, a religious victory that would result eventually in historic vindication. The kingdom of God might eventually be realized if only they remained faithful to that God whose name was One. Suffering was viewed as a prelude to eventual triumph over one's adversaries. "As the olive does not give of its precious oil except through adversity, so Israel does not bring forth its highest virtues except through adversity." (*Exodus Rabbah*) Outside pressures and common protective needs encouraged the Jew to band closely together in an invincible national cultural solidarity.

Religious symbols became an important channel unifying the Jewish people with meaningful supports for the group's conscious and unconscious need for identification. Ritual, both in the home and synagogue, was a vital factor in promoting the coalescence of a people. It helped them to belong and to communicate their common emotions through observances and practices. For many Jews, ritual became almost as concrete a representation of God as the graven image, Jesus. By utilizing a common object, one expressed kinship with the other. Religious symbols were his in-group community badge. These tokens created a sense of solidarity, of belongingness and of acceptance. The symbol was the same for all, definite and prescribed. In ritual one can love his co-religionist, because he does not strive against him and is not being striven against. A narcissistic identification was responsible for the ties that existed between members of the same group where they identified with one another because of one common characteristic: membership in the same minority ethnic group.

The synagogue became the nuclear and most important institution—the corporate attempt at group validation. The worship service with its instrumentality of organized singing, prayer, conscious moralizing and unconscious symbolism helped to bind the individual into the group. Its form of worship and associations complemented and invigorated the ordinary patterns of life. Together the Jews would read of the divine fiat of God's choice of the "holy seed" in contrast to those who would contend against the Lord's elect. In the synagogue, they would stand for the prayers and repeat: "Thou didst choose us (the Jews) for Thy service from among all peoples, loving us and taking delight in us. Thou didst exalt us above all tongues by making us holy through Thy commandments. Thou hast drawn us near, O Our King, unto Thy service and hast called us by Thy great and holy name." The worship would conclude with the liturgy: "God hath not made us like unto the heathens of the earth, nor fashioned us like the godless of the land; that He hath not made our destiny as theirs, nor cast our lot with their multitude.'' The doctrinal affirmation and spiritual conviction that the Jews were the Chosen People elected by God to serve Him was rooted deeply into the bedrock of Jewish ideology.

Of course, this concept was not indigenous to the Jews. Similar claims were found in the writings of the Italians, Chinese, Slavs, Japanese, English and others. However, for the Jew, the belief was a resolution of his own internal conflicts and feeling of inadequacy by exalting himself over his enemies. His frustrations often lead to an aggressive attitude toward all the Christians who were now regarded as actual or potential frustrators. ''For he who conceives himself hated by another,'' wrote Spinoza, ''and believes that he has given him no cause for hatred will hate that other in return.''

By translating the persecution of his people into evidence of the majority group's sense of their own inferiority, the Jew defended himself against his foes. Being the constant source of loathing, the Jew invented his own plausible excuses and alibis to explain his privations, deprivations and external frustrations. His defensive armor involved the stereotyping of the outside world as ''ignorant,'' ''obtuse,'' and ''subordinate.'' ''There must be a certain something about me that made the Christian so frightened,'' he thought. In order to preserve his inner self-respect, he expressed a sense of superiority and pre-eminence over the *goyishe kup* (the non-Jew's inadequacies). Jews would then resolve the protean world of common experience into two separate monoliths, with everything Jewish being depicted as divine and everything Gentile derided as demonic. The synagogue became more than a *Beth Tefillah* (House of Prayer). It was also a *Beth Hakenesseth* (House of Meeting). This was the place to laugh and live more comfortably and make fun of oneself and feel superior by scorning the persecutors, who are not "Mine (God's) own treasure from among all peoples." (Exodus 19:5–6)

The Jew often claimed a supremacy of faith: "Ours is the best!" . . . "Christianity borrowed from Judaism, you know!" . . . "How more rational and scientific is ours!" In many cases, the magnifications were but mere overstatements which masked his real rebellion and antagonism toward Judaism. The original feeling of disdain was derogated and its opposite was socially rewarded.

A reaction-formation is employed when an unconscious, painful trait is overcome by an exaggeration of its opposite socialized trait. For example, oversolicitude is the conscious response to an unconscious hate. Usually, this adaptation is an over-reaction in an effort to keep under control conscious, aggressive and terrifying impulses and urges.

Irrational exaggerations and extravagant claims disguised the Jew's antagonism toward his own faith. In order to escape the self-rejection inherent in his own anti-Semitism, he resorted to reaction-formation and became a militant champion of the Jews. Resentment of Judaism was frequently rendered unconscious by an overemphasis upon his love of the Jewish people. The ego was protected from the threatened repressed emotions by conscious feelings of love, protection, tenderness and gentleness.

Another method of coping with the outside world is compromise. In the compromise mechanism, the unacceptable impulse is not discharged directly because of resistances but released in a middle ground between complete satisfaction and complete dissatisfaction. One and the same symptom serves both to express and to inhibit the action. An example of compromise is a verbal criticism which is the mid-point between physical aggression and non-aggression.

A form of compromise frequently used by the Jew was humor. It involved the adaptation of the psyche in a compromise between the release of inhibition of unacceptable wishes, particularly in the desire to injure or to hurt, and the release of so-called play pleasure (the pleasure of thinking and acting like a child). Humor served as an outlet to the Jew for the expression of a variety of feelings that were inhibited and could not be expressed openly and directly. Action could be expressed and yet inhibited through humor. Freud believed humor was like dreaming because it gratified some wish-fulfillment which was unacceptable to the consciousness.

In their article, *Marginality and Jewish Humor,* Rosenberg and Shapiro noted that for the Jew, humor was often the badge and by-product of his own peculiar marginality and ambivalence, that satiric and yet schizophrenic observation of his own fate, the caricature of his own self-image. By telling disdainful stories about his own people, and especially those who had a different mode of behavior such as Orthodox Jews with their long tunics and curls, the stereotyped jokes by the Jews were often more acrimonious and barbed than those told by the worst anti-Semite. The raconteur was gratified by the laughter. His anxiety was relieved by the reinforcement of others sharing similar sentiments. The group's mutual identification was enhanced by sharing interpersonal tensions.

Humor was also extrapunitive by placing the responsibility outside of the self. It was a humor founded on the human trait of enjoying seeing someone else get the worst of it. The minority-conscious Jew expressed his hostility in humor by turning the tables on the aggressor, the *goy,* the contemptuous term for Gentiles. Contempt is a complex emotion compounded of envy, fear and emotional rejection.

One healthy mechanism of defense is sublimation. This adaptation alludes to the deflection of energy into intellectual, cultural or artistic pursuits. Primitive, unacceptable impulses are sublimated into socially acceptable activities and permitted freedom to flow into the consciousness without anxiety.

Respect for learning was one of the most effective ways to channel and deflect the inner conflicts of life in Judaism. In the face of discrimination and adversity, the redoubling of one's efforts in intellectual pursuits was a healthy response to a difficulty. Throughout the centuries, Jews were able to meet the handicap of anti-Semitism by the dynamic of Jewish living—education. It was as if to say: "If I am not accepted by the Christians, I will at least let them know that I am every bit as good as they, maybe better." Like the legendary case of Demosthenes who overcame his stuttering and became a famous orator, Jewish parents would urge their children to study and work harder in order to run the unequal race.

Study was also employed in Judaism as a method of separating the son from the mother, causing the lad to identify with the father. When the son was three or four years of age, the father assumed complete responsibility for the child and his education. Instruction was exclusively the province of the father and the male world. As soon as the boy began to learn, the prestige not only of the son but the father as well, increased in proportion to the child's advancement in his studies. If the son was a particularly astute youngster, he could participate in the debates of the men concerning a Talmudic point. Even bearded Jews would not be ashamed to make an appointment with him to pose a weighty question. Thus, the boy in Judaism identified with the male world at an early age. Community customs of separating the boy's mother (even before the development of the Oedipal Stage) helped to induce identification with the paternal elders, the father, and Father-God.

In attempting to conform to the high standards of his father, the son often experienced feelings of anxiety, fearing he might do something to snap the tenuous bond between them. Anxiety resulted from the intrapsychic conflict between the natural need for the child to gratify his own drives and the fear that if he did satisfy them, he might lose his father's acceptance. In addition, there was the apprehension of an infliction of physical pain or injury. In the *cheder* (Hebrew School), the male teacher stood as the substitute for the father. At the least provocation, erring students received a sharp blow with a stick. Even today, many Jewish fathers can recall having their knuckles severely rapped. Adherence to learning was maintained by the Jewish father or male surrogate through the real threat of bodily harm and fear of injury to the prized organs (Castration complex).

Since the Jew could find satisfaction only away from the hostile environment, he fled from the bitterness of the outside world into a universe entirely of his own, with emphasis on education. (The synagogue is also called a *Beth Hamidrash,* a House of Learning.) For his Judaism was the religion of Torah. The commandment: "You shall be My treasured possession among all the peoples" was understood to mean: "You, the sons of Israel, shall distinguish yourselves by devotion to God and through the means of learning." Did not Rabbi Joshua B. Levi assert that it was permissible to sell a synagogue in order to acquire a school? *Talmud Torah,* knowledge of God's word, had from ancient time been the Jew's way of saying: "Speak God, and like our ancestors at Sinai, we will do and we will hearken."

Joseph Caro (1555) wrote his *Shulchan Aruch* (Code of Jewish Law) reemphasizing the meticulous regulation of religious life. Meir, son of Baruch ha-Levi, Chief Rabbi of Vienna, had already innovated the system of ordination which conferred upon the holder, the title *Morenu* (our teacher) and with it the prerogative to exercise rabbinical functions. One joy in an environment of hate that could not be denied the Jew was *yichus* (the nobility of background, tradition and knowledge). Since he would not die, the Jew had his choice of an alternative: he had to cultivate a compensating culture or take the gamble of going stark crazy. With other peoples, learning was an after thought, a by-product of normal living or an entertainment for leisure hours. With the Jew it was a precondition for a sound mind. Long before the ghetto awoke to its daily routine, the student was already chanting his lesson. Long after the members of the ghetto slept, his candle still flickered. The bare bench was often his bed; his ragged coat, the pillow. This was the way of life, foretold in Jewish law: "This is the way of instruction. A morsel with salt shalt thou eat, and water in limited measure shalt thou drink; on the ground shalt thou sleep, and a life of hardship shalt thou live as in the Torah thou toilest. But if so thou doest, happy shalt thou be and it shall be well with thee. Aye, happy in this world, and well with thee in the world to come."

For the Jew in Austria, Judaism was perpetuated through the tradition-esteemed instrumentality of education. At the circumcision ceremony the prayer was invoked: "May he be raised for the *Torah,* for the *wedding,* and for doing good deeds." Juxtaposition of the words *Torah* and *wedding* was more than a coincidence. The dowry of the girl (wedding) was proportionate to the scholarship (Torah) of the prospective bridegroom. Affluent Jews would go to the *Yeshiva* and seek from the head of the theological school the best student for a possible son-in-law. To allow the pupil to continue his studies further, the wife often assumed the economic responsibilities of the family. In Jewish tradition, learning served as an historic token of prestige as well as an opportunity for a better marriage and increased wealth.

Education was also revered and respected in that it aided the Jew in an overcrowded ghetto to look inward to a life of contemplative content away from the myriad forms of oppression. Erudition suggested a belief in the omnipotence of thought, similar to the primitive concept of the child who assumed that his wishes and thoughts might govern the course of events in the outside world. Emphasis on learning as a means of control was especially strong during persecution.

Ghettos accentuated both the psychological and physical separation of Jew and Christian. In truth, the Jew was more at ease with his own people and could more readily carry through the group's distinctive attitudes and needs. A body of customs could be maintained and transferred almost intact from one generation to another. Many Jews considered it a divine command to practice separateness. This group gloried in every opportunity to raise the historic barriers higher and higher. In matters of religious practice, they would pit symbol against symbol and rite against rite. At the request of the Jewish population in 1624, Ferdinand II granted a suburb of Vienna as a place of residence for the Jews to be with their own kind. At first the section was called *Untere Werd,* later to be known as Leopoldstadt. This densely populated area was to become the home of Sigmund Freud. An undisturbed residence in Vienna was desired by the Jewish community so that it could serve as an impregnable rock against the outrages of the time. The family hearth was the antidote to the cruel, outside world. For the Jew, the eternal fugitive, the theme was *alles für die kinder* (everything for the children). Education was emphasized as the hope for an improved condition in the future.

Not every Jew could be a scholar in understanding the subtlety of the Talmudic prescriptions. Not all Jews were intellectuals. For those not so metaphysically endowed, an escape from the reality of the time arose.

Before the Freudian Era, a movement was led by a man who represented the complete opposite of cold pedantry. This new approach followed the uprisings in the Ukraine when more than 100,000 Jews lost their lives in less than a decade. Israel ben Eliezer, generally known by the name of Israel Baal Shem Tov (1700-1760), brought forth an interpretation of Judaism based not upon reason but faith; not upon intellect but emotion. In his movement of Chassidism, a man could literally escape his unbearable miseries by immersing himself in a mystical *hithlahabuth* (the esoteric kindling of the soul with God). To the masses who hungered for a direct, simple, stimulating religion which they could follow without any philosophical sophistications, the doctrine of salvation through prayer and humility rather than study was appealing. The unsuppressed emotions and optimistic Chassidic spirit served as a buffer against the depressing environment of dissolution and terror.

It is important to note that many of the pioneers in psychoanalysis were born of parents upon whom

Chassidism had made an impact. Freud acknowledged his father, Jakob, came from Chassidic stock even as Josef Breuer's father was a Chassidic rabbi. Professor David Bakan postulated that Freud gave birth to psychoanalysis because his mind was already pregnant with Chassidic mysticism. He mentioned Freud's awareness of the sixteenth century Jewish mystical physician, Solomon Almoli, whose book *The Solution of Dreams* gives a description of sexual symbolism, wish fulfillment and word play as elements found in dreams. Many counterparts of Freudian theory were found in the Zohar (literally *brightness,* the mystical writings issued in part by Moses de Leon in the fourteenth century) such as the portrayal of primordial man where the divine act of creation was given an erotic character and where sex relations were treated as avenues of salvation. There were the common attributes of oral transmission, mysticism, revelation, and deification of the leader. E. Steindletz also mentioned the prior belief of Chassidism in an unconscious sex drive and pleasure principle. Steindletz is, however, not prepared to accept Bakan's thesis that psychoanalysis was a scientific secularization of Chassidism and maintained that despite the similarity, the conclusions each one draws are mutually contradictory. Nevertheless, many rabbis and psychologists continue to discuss the relationships between Freud, modern psychoanalytic thought and the mystical movement of Chassidism.

Until the end of the eighteenth century, Austrian Jews continued to live a life of their own, segregated from the surrounding peoples by restrictive laws imposed from without, and by the need for defensive solidarity felt from within. Greatly in need of an explanation to allay its fears and a scapegoat upon whom to thrust its hostilities, town after town turned on the Jews. The story is told of two Austrians who were reading an official bulletin. "I see where another anti-Jewish campaign begins on Monday," said one. The other replied, "That means another wage cut on Saturday." They knew from experience that if conditions worsened sufficiently to necessitate another reduction in wages, the blame would again be placed upon the Jews.

With the same pernicious design, the feudal lords and Church authorities drove the "culpable" Jews from the land and from the trades. Segregation in turn encouraged further discriminations, for the Jews were strangers and there was a dislike of the unlike. Fantastic charges were leveled. It was charged that Jews murdered Christian children for ritualistic purposes and, by poisoning the wells, caused the pestilence which devastated the unsanitary cities of the period. Some Jews met these appalling situations by turning inward to intellectual activities and mysticism. Others found the baptismal font to be the touchstone of protection from the assaults of the anti-Semites. Some even rallied to the irresistible appeal of a man called Sabbatai Zevi with his messianic pretensions and to his successor, Jacob Frank (1750), the "incarnation" of David, Elijah, Jesus and Mohammed.

At the end of the eighteenth century—heralded as the age of rationalism and the Renaissance of intellectual activity—new developments were to take place. As a symbol of this era Gotthold Lessing, the great German non-Jewish writer, gave to his play *Nathan the Wise* (1779) the Gospel of Tolerance. Nathan, the central character, was molded after Lessing's friend, Moses Mendelssohn, who in Lessing's opinion possessed every attribute of wisdom, kindness and nobility. Said the Friar: "Nathan! Nathan! You are a Christian!" To which Nathan the Jew retorted: "We are of one mind! For that which makes me, in your eyes, a Christian, makes you, in my eyes, a Jew." Moses Mendelssohn, Lessing's friend, eventually became known as the "German Socrates." In addition to his own philosophic works, he translated the Torah into a lyric prose with commentary that added new insights to those Jews who had so long been confined to physical and mental ghettos. At Mendelssohn's request, Christian Wilhelm Dohm, the Prussian Councilor of State, even published a plea for Jewish emancipation in which he discussed the deplorable conditions of the Jews and argued that if the Jews had faults, many of these were the result of Christian oppression. Life was changing, thanks to the genius of Voltaire and Rousseau, of Goethe and Pope, of Spinoza and Mendelssohn.

Even before the French Revolution, the Austrian Emperor Joseph II, an admirer of Voltaire and a disciple of the school of enlightenment, issued a revolutionary series of laws in 1781 relating to the Jews—an Edict of Toleration. Joseph said: "I love humanity without limitation," and "It is time to make the Jews useful to the state." He abolished the Jewish *Leibmaut* (poll-tax and double court and chancellery taxes), the

Jewish badge, and granted the Jews complete freedom of movement in Vienna as well as the right to choose their own occupations and attend the public and normal schools. The Emperor promoted what he called "philosophical morality." All adults and their children were forced to learn the language of the country, since he decreed that in the future only documents written in that idiom could possess legal force.

Jews were suddenly catapulted from the medievalism of the past toward a new, unexpected modernity. After the fall of the Bastille on July 14, 1789, Jews made contact with the outside world and learned of sciences that had shattered ancient theologies and of a contemporary revolutionary faith called "Reason." Joseph II introduced a new type of Jew into Austrian society—*the Salon Jude.* The Salon Jew was not only tolerated but welcomed into the drawing rooms of the Christian intelligentsia. Discussions were not about religion or Talmud but literature and philosophy. So cataclysmic was this change for the Jew, that no prior preparation could be made. Of course, not all the Jews were affected. Many could not comprehend the Newtonian physics or the speculative thoughts of John Locke. For some, there were the lingering loyalties to the ghetto, the Torah, and to the God of Antiquity. For others who were now freely participating in the business of the new industrial revolution, there was a kind of "religious" devotion to the state that had allowed the Jew the mobility to move upward on the ladder of wealth.

The nineteenth century of Sigmund Freud could be characterized by the motto *Sapere Aude*—Dare to know. Learning remained a unique trait identified with the Jewish ethos. Education continued as a badge of honor, a stamp of nobility that provided an aid toward a forward thrust in the status system. But there was one significant difference—it was a different kind of learning. No longer did the search for Judaism keep pace with the whetted thirst for general knowledge. Even the approaches were different. In the past, the learned Jew had little interest in pure science, pure literature, or pure poetry. He could see no *taklis* (object) —no direct goal if the subject matter did not pertain to the Jewish people or everyday life. Mathematics was studied in connection with architectural or agricultural problems; aesthetics in relationship to applied arts or the beautification of the synagogue; and philosophy in direct correlation with ethics and the understanding of God. Historically, the preoccupation with learning had welded Judaism and life into an indissoluble union. The new engrossment with science did not!

A type of erudition developed which, instead of blending with the traditional love of Judaism, quarreled with its ancient institutions. Science was set up as a god. Intellect was its prophet. This was the kind of rationalism which Sartre called "an avenue of flight (from Judaism). I may even say, the royal road of flight." The most passionate protagonist of reason was the Jew whose present was his only reality, and for whom there was no other fulfillment. The movement into rationalism became the attempt of some born of Jewish background to escape the Jewish world. Not only was the religious faith professionally embarrassing for many, but the spiritual elements were bereft of meaning. No longer could answers be accepted on faith. Many now questioned the ancient values and assumptions incorporated in their religious theologies and as a result became agitated and disturbed.

These new scholars were seeking a catholicity of truth as opposed to the particularisms of any one sect or religion. Though the Jews were to produce great intellectuals—Freud in medicine, Einstein in physics, Marx in economics—there were relatively few contributors to music, literature, and art. Dimont's answer is that the Jews as outsiders could not give expression to the normative Christian cultural milieu as did a Beethoven, Keats and Renoir. "The abstractions of Spinoza, Marx, Freud, Einstein are universal, not identifiable expressions of a creed." Dimont explained further that some Jews did aspire for worldwide acclaim and subsequently felt compelled to join other faiths for reasons that excluded religious conviction.

For Karl Ludwig Börne (orginally Löb Baruch), the famous literary and political writer, his conversion to the Lutheran faith in 1818 had no religious significance. Conversion was his frank attempt to solidify his position as a critic of the German people whom he wished to exhort not as a Jew but as a true countryman. (Börne later became the favorite author of Freud and his books remained the only volumes that Sigmund retained from his adolescent years.) Heinrich Heine, poet, journalist, and literary critic (1791–1856) was another who believed that his baptism was but a "ticket of admission" to his culture. Like other intellectuals before and after his time, his spiritual fervor was channeled to a faith for all of humanity, with liberty and justice for all. Ironically, because of his Jewish origin, his native city of Düsseldorf later refused permission to have a sculptured memorial erected to him. Despite his conversion to Christianity, the Nazis burned his books. Since it was impossible to remove his *Lorelei*—so great was its popularity—Heine's name (since he was born a Jew) was obliterated and replaced by the words, "Author Unknown."

Multitudes of Jews did convert in the nineteenth and twentieth centuries for a variety of reasons. Especially the materially and "socially elect" abandoned the tradition for the majority faith. Friedrich Julius Stahl (originally Schlesinger), a noted jurist (1802–1861), demonstrated his own emancipation from Judaism as leader of the political Conservative Party by writing the Tivoli program which voiced dissent with any emancipation of his former co-religionists. A great volume of Jews flirted with the possibility of embracing Christianity including such well-known personalities as Sigmund Freud in 1886 and Franz Rosenzweig in 1913.

The Jewish Utopia was short-lived. Increased opposition toward the end of Joseph's reign forced him to withdraw most of his reforms. He died in 1790 a disappointed and broken man. Nevertheless Joseph's fame was so highly renowned that by the turn of the nineteenth century, Jews continued to immigrate and constituted ten per cent of Vienna's population. Despite the succeeding reactionary regimes of Leopold II (1790–1792) and Francis I (1792–1835), the Edict of

Joseph II continued to stimulate interest not only among Jews but also among Christians. Men like Friedrich Klopstock, the eminent German poet, took up the cudgels of defense for Jews and all mankind. A small group of Jews continued to hope and believe that they might yet emancipate themselves from the onerous yoke of their faith by casting their lot with the new era of world brotherhood.

For the Jews as a whole, the threat of expulsion and danger continued. Prince Clemens Metternich, the Austrian minister to Emperor Ferdinand, formed the reactionary Holy Alliance which marked the reestablishment of the Christian state. The head of the state was to become the official head of the Church. Yet, the Viennese Jews clandestinely (officially, they were not permitted to organize) carried on philanthropic, religious and cultural affairs. Conditions improved somewhat with the Congress of Vienna of 1815, marked by the erection of a new synagogue in Vienna in 1826, and the liberal policies of Emperor Ferdinand I (1835–1848) who abolished the special Jewish oath. (This *Oath More Judaico* was administered to Jews while they were standing naked in a court of law. Its purpose was to degrade and humiliate the Jews and especially to discredit them when they participated in a suit against Christians.)

There was another ray of hope when the revolt of 1848 drove Metternich out of the country. Like the prior regime of Joseph II, the Revolution was said to herald the millennium. Jewish and Christian liberals fomented the uprising that was temporarily to abolish the ghettos, rescind Jewish taxes, and place a gray-bearded rabbi among the Christian deputies. The Jew's sympathy with liberal causes was understandable. When the country was liberated, he too would be free. He could easily sympathize with any underdog, though not of his faith, for he understood what it meant to feel the "slings and arrows of outrageous fortune." He could throw himself into the struggle for equality with tremendous vigor, since for every injustice corrected, he experienced deeply the satisfaction of a personal wrong redressed. Even those who ignored the ritualism of Judaism often felt their religion could best be expressed by the messianic fervor of social reform. Central to the development of a belief as a holy people was the concept of the Jews in a life of holiness serving God by means of moral conduct.

In 1848, the Vienna Jews had much to fear from the existing government's policy of repression. They joined the anti-Metternich revolt enthusiastically. The number who participated in the liberal uprising was large and influential. Included were Adolf Fischhof, the Viennese physician, who became the president of the police force. Joseph Goldmark, the chemist who had gained a seat in the Reichstag representing Vienna, served as a captain in the revolutionary army. At the first skirmish between students and military, five fell dead. Of these, two were Jews. All five were buried in a common grave. At the funeral, Rabbi Isaac Noah Mannheimer (1793–1865), allowed to speak before the Christian clergy, said: "You have wished that these dead Jews should rest with you in your earth, in the same earth. Do not begrudge it that those who have fought the same battle with you, a hard battle, should live with you upon the same earth, free and untroubled as yourselves."

After the revolution, the old discriminations were gradually restored again. An attack on liberal democracy was cloaked in anti-Jewish feeling. The new ruler, Emperor Ferdinand, sought to make the struggle for liberty appear detestable to the Austrians by representing it to be the work of the Jew. He, however, was too weak to remain at the helm of the state's ship and was replaced by his nephew, Francis Joseph I, who adopted autocratic policies. Total blame for the revolution and all objectionable phenomena was again thrust upon the Jews. Adolf Fischhof was arrested on charges of high treason. Goldmark was sentenced to death. A constitution proclaimed by the Emperor without the consent of the parliament was promulgated in 1849. Clergymen continued to agitate against any abolition of Austria's character as a Roman Catholic country. In 1850, they petitioned the Emperor not to appoint Jews to office. Once again the Jews saw themselves as routed in their forward advance. A Viennese lawyer, Dr. Heinrich Jacques, described the situation and said, in appealing to the reason of the ruling class: "By excluding its Jews from the rights of freedom of enterprise, the ownership of property, and the attainment of civil and political offices, Austria allows a substantial part of its material and spiritual national capital to lie idle. It makes of its Jews unproductive consumers instead of generally useful producers. Austria harms itself by driving the material capital of the Jews into cosmopolitan trade instead of identifying it with the fate of the Fatherland."

Another result of the abortive revolution was the

establishment of Czech nationalism as a factor in Austrian politics. The new chauvinism was first directed against the German-Austrians, the ruling class in Moravia and Bohemia. Soon the hatred was fanned against the Jews who were German in language and education. This was one of the developments that later forced Jakob Freud to leave Freiberg, Moravia, where the spoken tongue was Czech.

Despite the fact that the Jews were thwarted, there was one chief difference between the discomfited Jews of the Middle Ages and the frustrated Jews living in Austria in the 1850's. The latter had tasted too freely of liberty to accept its denial passively. Ludwig Börne expressed the sentiment: "I, as a slave from my birth, love liberty more than you (non-Jew); yea, because I was trained in servitude, I understand liberty better than you." Equally significant was a change in the internal institutional structure. Since the authority of the Jewish law in civil and criminal matters was replaced by the public courts of the state, Orthodox Judaism was deprived of its legal autonomy. In addition, a new generation of Jewish children who had never studied in a *cheder* (Jewish parochial school) rejected the mentality of the archaic Judaism of the old ghetto. The theory of evolution published in 1859 by Charles Darwin was in variance with the Biblical story of the origin of life. Many of the rabbis of the time denounced those who dared to challenge God's divine law but it was of little avail. As they read out of Judaism all who followed these new "heresies," assimilation occurred in great frequency, mostly confined to the upper echelons of the social scale.

With the Jew becoming aware of the outside world,

the degree of assimilation began to mount. (In Herbart's psychology, assimilation is the process of integrating the new experience into the apperceptive mass or background of relevant experiences.) For some Jews, there was more than just the need of mimicking the majority group, but the desire of merging into this dominant group. The expression, identification with the aggressor, was used to designate the method by which a person identified with the prohibitions and patterns of life established by a feared, authority figure. The purpose of this identification was to enable the aggrieved to avoid punishment by becoming obedient to the demands of the aggressor. Out of fear and self-enhancement, he not only imitated but incorporated the forces of the aggressor, the authority figure.

For many Jews of this period, there was a denial of all the Jewish ethnic, cultural, and religious traditions in the unconscious seeking of the Christian ethos. By identifying with the dominant group, he tried, vicariously, to appropriate their strength and power. Alexander de Tocqueville described the Negro and his identification with the aggressor which could bear a semblance to some Jews and their relationship with the anti-Semitic world. He said: "The Negro makes a thousand fruitless efforts to insinuate himself among men who repulse him. He conforms to the tastes of his oppressors, and adopts their opinions and hopes by imitating them to form a part of their community. Having been told from the beginning that his race is naturally inferior to that of the whites, he assents to the proposition and is ashamed of his own nature. In each of his features, he discovers a trace of slavery;

and if it were in his power, he would willingly rid himself of everything that makes him what he is."

The leap from the former isolation and segregation to the present sporadic integration brought other religious approaches. Some completely discarded the paraphernalia of the past and converted to Christianity. Others, however, sought to understand and interpret Judaism in a more modern expression. Leopold Zunz coined the expression, *Wissenschaft des Judentums* (Science of Judaism), a rational inquiry to enable the new generation to comprehend Judaism in intelligible and rational formulations. Abraham Geiger (1810–1874), Samuel Holdheim (1806–1860), and Isaac Noah Mannheimer (1793–1865) established a Reform Judaism based on the premise that Judaism was an evolving religion that must adapt itself to the needs of each generation rather than remain a closed, revealed faith whose immutability was circumscribed by God. Zacharias Frankel (1801–1875) offered a different orientation—the "positive historic Judaism"—which became the basis of Conservative Judaism. Entrenched Orthodox communities did not take this threat lightly. Rabbi Isaac Bernays, whose granddaughter, Martha, later became Freud's wife, condemned the Reform prayerbook of the Hamburg Temple and placed it under ban.

This factionalism only served to confuse and embitter the situation. There were other weighty questions that were more important than the internecine struggles of the rabbis. A decision had to be rendered for the first time in two millennia—ancestral sanctity or economic gain? Since his shop serviced Christians (no longer was his place of business confined to the

Jewish section), should the Jewish merchant's store stay open on the Sabbath and Holy Days or should it not? A familiar query arose: "Gold or God?" Former pride in being a Jew turned to bewilderment because of still another factor. Confusion was compounded when Jewish learning, that had so long existed in a vacuum of isolation, was now considered obsolete when compared with the music, art, and philosophy of the newly-discovered civilization. The native culture seemed so outmoded. Where ghetto life previously helped to unite the Jew into a communal setting, the new generation became a collection of cliques, academic societies, clans and miniscule sibs. For many, the synagogue was no longer the focus of Jewish life. The Jew felt a gap between his label and his own actuality, frequently an absence of authenticity. He was exposed to attrition, evaporation and particularly, perplexity. While there was a massive contribution by Jews to Austrian as well as to the larger secular life, there was now a glaring failure in the advancement of the cultural and religious life of Austrian Jewry.

But the Jew was not free. He was aware at an early age that he was different from his Christian neighbor, which brought an ever greater anxiety and tension. Choices between Jewish and non-Jewish alternatives in school and community gave clear evidence of culture conflict. Milton Steinberg noted that "It was pure perversity to continue to study Talmud when Shakespeare, Goethe, and Gibbon were available for the asking. Maimonides seemed hopelessly antiquated in comparison with Kant and Hegel." At the time that the Jew was developing a desire for wider contacts with non-Jews and a gradual absorption into the dominant culture, his ethnic group membership became an increasing source of strain. He was plagued by a vague self-image as to the meaning of being a Jew. His understanding of Jewish content was circumscribed. His confused parents often gave little direction.

Jakob Freud understood that if his son were to make his way successfully, Sigmund must be skilled in that learning of which the world approved. The child studied science while the father read the Bible. The son became intensely conscious of his biculturality which vacillated not only from generation to generation but moment to moment. Thus, a Jewish child was frequently in disagreement with the elders' views and was likely to regard the foreign accent and alien customs with some disfavor. Anxiety was heightened when he was perched uncomfortably between two cultures and often feeling a part of neither.

For the Jew in Austria was, in Freud's words, "proscribed from the compact majority." In the ambiguous smear of the inkblot, the Jew in Austria was the symbolic representation of such antithetical concepts as love and hate, dominance and submission, oversexuality and impotency, communism and capitalism. (Karl Marx, 1818–1883, was a Jew by birth.) The tragedy of the situation was personified in all its irony by Albert Einstein in an event of his early youth. At a gathering in one of the glittering salons in Paris, a lady sitting next to the lionized scientist posed the following question: "Professor, what can you tell me of your theory that I can understand?" "Well," replied the physicist with a good-natured smile, "it's all simple enough. If my theory proves to be correct, you, as a French lady, will assert that I am a Frenchman; if it proves incorrect, you will have me a Jew. Now, the Germans, should my theory prove correct, will claim me as a German; but if incorrect, they will maintain I am a Jew. You see everything is relative and conditional." In the response, Einstein gave an example of relativity, not in the cosmic sphere, but in the social and political world of prejudice and defense.

The precarious, minority position of the Jew in the non-Jewish world often led him to strenuous, even extravagant efforts of self-validation. The familiar motto, *Nemo me impugne lacessit,* expressed the thought: No one attacks me and gets away with it! For some there might be the retaliation against society with extropunitive behavior as prejudice against the out-group, continual suspicion and obsessive concern. Or the sensitization could evoke the intropunitive posturing of hatred of one's faith. Were Judaism not to exist, then he would not have been singled out for ridicule and derision. He might have disdain for himself or at least that part of him that is Jewish. Kurt Lewin likened the lot of the Jew to the condition of adolescents who were never quite certain whether they would be admitted to the dominant adult world. The Jew, he said, was comparable to the adolescent, belonging neither here nor there—a marginal being. He was to live on two levels: a member of the general community and as a son of the covenant. He was in this world but was never quite of it.

To understand the life of Sigmund Freud as a Jew in Austria, the following story may be worth volumes of philosophizing. It is about Georg Brandes, the famous literary critic and historian, who related it about himself in his *Recollections of My Childhood and Youth*:

"When I dragged behind the nursemaid who held my younger brother by the hand, sometimes I heard a shout behind me, and if I turned around would see a grinning boy, making faces and shaking his fist at me. For a long time I took no particular notice, but as time went on I heard the shout oftener and asked the maid what it meant. 'Oh, nothing!' she replied. But on my repeated asking she simply said: 'It is a bad word.'

"But one day, when I had heard the shout again, I made up my mind that I would know, and when I came home asked my mother: 'What does it mean?'

" 'Jew!' said mother. 'Jews are people.'

" 'Nasty people?'

" 'Yes,' said mother, smiling, 'sometimes very ugly people, but not always.'

" 'Could I see a Jew?'

" 'Yes, very easily,' said mother, lifting me quickly in front of the large oval mirror above the sofa.

"I uttered a shriek, so that mother hurriedly put me down again, and my horror was such that she regretted not having prepared me."

For Freud, as with Brandes and other Jewish children growing up in an atmosphere where they were *persona non grata,* life was an angry bully, making faces, shaking a menacing fist and shouting names. But Sigmund, like his hero Hannibal, would not be intimidated; he faced his tormenters and shook his fist right back. He was a thrice-homeless man: a revolutionary scientist among Austrians, an Austrian among Germans, and a Jew among the people of the world. Yet he refused to be bound by the fetters of a hostile society. Rising above prejudice, he was able to expend his energy in an exploration into a bold, hitherto undiscovered field, to the benefit of his tormentors and all mankind.

II. THE ESSENCE OF JEWISHNESS

In the preface to the Hebrew edition of *Totem and Taboo,* Freud asserted that he did not understand Hebrew, that he was estranged from the religion of his Jewish forbears and that he was unable to share the belief in the nationalistic ideals of Zionism. Yet, he could not and would not disavow being Jewish, even though his religious heritage was a supreme obstacle to his recognition and acceptability. Freud observed: "I might, in all reserve, submit the question whether my own personality as a Jew did not have some share in the antipathy which the world at large felt toward psychoanalysis."

He asserted, however, that he would remain loyal to his people. Were someone to ask him: "What is still Jewish in you after you abandoned all those things common to your people?" Freud could only respond: "Still very much, perhaps, the main part of my personality." He admitted that he would be unable to put this thought into clear words, and added: "It will certainly someday become accessible to scientific investigation."

Even though he was not religious, Freud believed that he was a Jew in his deepest nature and that he had maintained a great deal of what being Jewish meant—"probably its very essence." Freud did not amplify this statement, and one can only conjecture what he meant by "probably its very essence." Perhaps he referred to his deep regard for those values emphasized in the child-rearing practices of the Jewish home, such as the concern with family life. The Jewish home was regarded as the *Mikdash Me'at* (the miniature sanctuary) where the husband and wife were priest and priestess. This kindred solidarity constituted the basis of Jewish life and increased in cohesiveness when confronted with discrimination. Throughout history, Freud noted, Jews placed the highest value upon the family. "Jewish family life," he said, "is on a higher plane than that of the non-Jew." Freud's own home life was kept indissoluble by his deep affection for his wife and children. In Lionel Trilling's words: "An heroic English puritanism joined with the ancient idea of public virtue and confirmed the morality of Freud's Jewish home and helped form the young man's notion of how a life must be lived: with sternness, fortitude, and honor."

Freud's "essence of Judaism" could also relate to preoccupation with learning. In the past two millennia, education was the pivotal center of Jewish life for a people scattered over the face of the earth with no political state or authoritarian institutions binding them together. Knowledge received the highest priority. It was more important than priesthood or royalty. As the great Hillel remarked: "An ignoramus cannot be truly pious." Ideals of learning helped keep the Jewish people on a high cultural and intellectual plane. A. A. Brill discussed this essence of Freud's Judaism: "I felt that his Jewish descent—constitution—and his later experiences—environment—played a great part in the molding of his character, and in directing his future interests. He had an inordinate curiosity for knowledge and a stubborn perseverence in the pursuance of the same. To be sure, a strong desire for knowledge is no Jewish monopoly, but he did come from a people who even long before the diaspora were wont to drum into their male children that 'Knowledge is better than pearls.' "

Freud may also have experienced the "essence of Judaism" through his community activities with other Jews. Many of his important theories were delivered before the Fraternity of Jewish Students and the B'nai B'rith organization. Most of the colleagues in his movement were Jewish, including Alfred Adler, Wilhelm Stekel, Max Kahane, Rudolph Reitler, Fritz Wittels, Karl Abraham, Siegfried Bernfeld, Melanie Klein, Rudolph Loewenstein, Barbara Low, Van d'Chys, Sandor Ferenczi, A. A. Brill, Otto Rank, Paul Federn, Josef Breuer, A. J. Storfer, Wilhelm Fliess and Theodor Reik. But whatever the reasons—historical, sociological, psychological—group bonds did provide a warm shelter from the outside world. In social relations with other Jews, informality and familiarity formed a kind of inner security, a "we-feeling," illustrated even by the selection of jokes and stories recounted within the group. It is what Freud called "the clear awareness of an inner identity, the secret of the same inner construction."

Freud's concepts were to some extent motivated by his interpretation of the essence of his being. True, Freud was first and foremost a scientist, largely responsible for introducing a breath of fresh air into the musty, dry-as-dust atmosphere of nineteenth century academic psychology. His store houses of theories and hypotheses will keep researchers busy for many years to come. His psychoanalysis, as a totality, presented a very complex structure comprising a technique of therapy, a body of evidence, and an observational method articulated at varying degrees of abstraction and generalization. But Freud, though a scientist, was also a man of flesh and blood. No man works in a vacuum. He lived in an era where he and his people were ostracized, boycotted, hedged about with restriction, confined to concentration camps and even murdered. He affirmed that the main part of his personality was Jewish and never denied that, as a Jewish scientist living in anti-Semitic Austria, he had his own religio-racial conflicts to resolve which colored his thinking and beliefs. Many of his views derived from his culture—from Vienna at the turn of the century. Both Kardiner and Roheim believed that the specific attitudes Freud elucidated were closely related to his own faith, family and society.

Understandably, the greatest criticism of this creative thinker emanated from Christian rather than from Jewish circles. Some have attributed the Jews' relative acceptance of psychiatry to the fact that theology and doctrine play a lesser role in Judaism than in Christianity. Emphasis in Judaism is not placed upon creed but deed. Reason is of primacy. Medieval Jewish philosophers stressed the idea that knowledge—all knowledge—is vital; it is the pillar of our very being. Faith without reason is mute.

Still another authority, Samuel Z. Klausner suggests that the Jewish assent of psychiatry is due to the "Jewish elements in Freud's thought and movement. Freud himself was a Jew, and most of the members of his immediate Vienna circle were Jews. Admittance to the psychoanalytic movement required analysis by a previous initiate, a sort of 'apostolic succession.' The original Jewish group tended to analyze Jews. Unwittingly, psychoanalytic ideology may be couched in a Jewish ethic strange to individuals socialized in the Protestant ethic."

Even the sexual aspect of Freud's doctrines which had so alarmed the Christian world was in harmony with the Jewish viewpoint. Judaism maintains that if one denies himself the physical enjoyments of love, he also denies the spiritual potential within him. The sexual love relationship is a high adventure of the human spirit; an opportunity for a man and woman to make a oneness of their separateness. One does not thwart his body, but rather sanctifies it through love. Voluntary abstinence from sexual relations in marriage is a triple sin—against the health of the body, the fulfillment of soul, and the welfare of society.

Freud emphasized man's biological nature. He connected the psychosexual phenomenon with the universal physical need to avoid pain by enjoying pleasure. Henry Enoch Kagan, the rabbi-psychologist, compared this approach with that found in Christianity: "Judaism is not burdened as is Christianity with Paulinian derogations of sex. The way of a man with a maid . . . is very realistic and wholesome to the writer of the *Song of Songs*. The creative value of the sexual motive was recognized by the rabbis in their well-known formula that were it not for the *Yetzer Ra* (evil inclination) men would not build homes. Even the feminine-masculine pattern, the factor of bi-sexuality in each person is implied in the Creation account that 'male and female made He them.' And Freud's effort to relate the libidinal with the rational, to see civilization as a sublimation of its sexual discontents recalls the Hebrew verb *Yoda* which stands for both knowledge and the experience of sex. Freud himself alluded to this Biblical origin of his thought when he wrote '*Erkennen* (knowledge) means *Coitiren* (coitus) in the Bible.' "

Thus, we see that out of the context of history, environment, and the genius of mind emerged a man and a creative thinker. The influence of the traumatic life's circumstances upon Freud's holistic, total personality and thought is indisputable. Dr. Robert Elliott, writing in the *Journal of the Perkins School of Theology,* asserted: "Religious people have been tempted to play footsie with Jung because he makes religious noises, while Freud makes atheistic noises. But I am convinced that Jung presents a viewpoint profoundly antithetical to a Biblical and Christian anthropology. In contrast, Freud is practically an Old Testament man in the flesh."

Freud persisted in maintaining his Jewish selfhood. He retained the essence of his faith and hearkened through blood and tears to the wise master of *Proverbs:* "Remove not the ancient landmark which your fathers have set" and make loyalty a signet seal of thy faith. He was proud of his heritage. He was like the

Gaon Saadiah who a thousand years before saw the sufferings of his people and said: Anyone who ridicules us because of our faith, and who thinks us fools for enduring so much when we could readily find happiness by leaving the fold is truly lacking in understanding. He may be compared with a man who observes the sowing of precious seeds of grain for the first time. Such a man would laugh at anyone whom he saw toiling to throw the seeds out over a field. He would not understand that the harvest would follow, and bring in many times more precious food than that which has been cast out.

III. SIGMUND FREUD, HIS RELIGION AND HIS WORLD

1856 The scene was Freiberg, a small town in Moravia, part of an Austro-Hungarian empire that was beginning to decay. In the village of 5,000 Germans and Czechs, ninety-six per cent of the population were Roman Catholics and two per cent were Jews. Citizens of the community spoke Czech while the Jews spoke German and Yiddish. Anti-Semitism was rampant. The Concordat of August 18th delivered all of Austria into the hands of the clericals. Jews were excluded from positions as teachers in elementary and high-schools while the children were barred from public schools. Jewish house-physicians in the Vienna hospitals were limited in number. Authorities ordered all Jews "who have sneaked into Christian real estate to be removed." These restrictions aimed at maintaining Catholic influence in Austria.

In this setting in the year 1856 a child was born at 117 Schlossergasse in the town of Freiberg. Originally the family came from Buczacz, a town to the east of Stanislav in Galicia. The great-grandfather of the infant was Rabbi Ephraim Freud; the grandfather, Rabbi Schlomo Freud; and the father, Jakob Freud. Jakob was born at Tysmenitz in 1815 and lived until the age of 81 years. A wool merchant, he was married twice: first in 1832, with two sons, Emanuel and Philip, resulting from the union. In 1855 he married Amalia Nathanson, a slender and pretty young girl of 16. She was the descendant of a famous Talmudic scholar, the eighteenth-century Nathan Halevy Charmatz of Brody, Poland. Interestingly enough the rabbi who officiated at their wedding was Noah Mannheimer, a leader in the Jewish Reform Movement who later participated in a polemic against Rabbi Isaac Bernays (the grandfather of the girl this couple's son would someday marry).

Of course, the boy is known to all of us as Sigmund Freud, named in Hebrew, Schlomo, for his paternal grandfather who died three months before the grandchild's birth. The text of the Gedenkblatt, certificate of birth and circumcision, reads: "My son Schlomo Sigismund, long may he live, was born on the third day, the first of year 5664, 6:30 P.M. on May 6th, (1)856, and was inducted into the covenant on the third day, the 8th of Iyar, on May 13, 1856. The Mohel (circumciser) was Shimshon Frankel of Ostrau; the patron was Reb Lippe, together with his sister, Mirel Hurwitz, the children of the Rabbi of Czernowitz. The Sandek (godfather) was Reb Shmuel of Vienna. (Done) here Freyberg (Freiberg)."

Schlomo's name was entered into the registry office as Sigismund, presumably because of his parents' great admiration for Sigismund, the tolerant Polish monarch who lived between 1467 and 1548. Not until he was 22 did Freud change the name to Sigmund, perhaps to sound more Austro-German than Slav. One psychoanalyst equated this change to the old Jewish tradition of altering the name of a person seriously ill in order to cheat the *Malach Hamoves* (the Angel of Death). A dying person might be given the name *Chayim* (Life) or *Alter* (Old) hoping to confuse the Angel of Death and perhaps influence positively the individual's future destiny. "The change of name has the symbolic significance of death and resurrection," noted Maryse Choisy. In compliance with Freud's wishes, the name Sigmund was adopted by his family and friends.

As we have seen, then, Sigmund was born to a family where the mother, Amalia, was half the age of the father, Jakob, a widower with two sons at the time of his second marriage. At the time of birth, Sigmund was not only the child of a very young mother and a middle-aged father, but the uncle of a nephew who was one year older than himself. Though subsequently seven other children were born to Amalia, Sigmund, the eldest, always remained the mother's favorite.

"My parents were Jews, and I have remained a Jew myself," Sigmund later wrote in his *Autobiographical Study*. Concerning his origin, he stated that he had reason to believe that his father's family was settled for a long period at Cologne but fled eastwards as a result of the persecutions of the Jews during the 14th or 15th century. In the course of the 19th century they migrated from Lithuania through Galicia into German-Austria. His father, Jakob, born of Chassidic stock, believed the Bible to be inspired by God, with contents unique and unparalleled.

Martin Freud reminisced about his grandparents (Sigmund's parents): "I saw my grandmother Amalia often. Grandmother came from East Galicia, then still part of the Austrian Empire. It might not be known by many people that Galician Jews were a peculiar race, not only different from any other races inhabiting Europe, but absolutely different from Jews who had lived in the West for some generations. They, these Galician Jews, had little grace and no manners; and their women were certainly not what we should call ladies.

"Memorable occasions were the family gatherings in Amalia's flat. These were on Christmas Day and New Year's Eve, for Amalia ignored Jewish feasts. And, finally, something about my mother's ancestry. She came from a family of intellectuals. Two of her uncles were well-known men of letters and her grandfather had been the Chief Rabbi of Hamburg, a personage who had gained historical importance amongst the Jewish people of that city, where he was known as *chochem* (the wise one).

"Grandmother Emmeline was a much less vital personage than Amalia, but to us she was a character, too, and I remember her fairly well. She was an Orthodox Jewess, a practicing one, who hated and despised gay Vienna. True to the severe regulations of the Orthodox Jewish law, she wore the *scheitel* (wig) which was crowned with two close-fitting artificial plaits. She stayed with us occasionally, and on Saturdays we used to hear her singing Jewish prayers in a small but firm and melodious voice. All of this, strangely enough in a Jewish family, seemed alien to us children who had been brought up without any instruction in Jewish ritual."

Sigmund's niece, Judith Heller, recalled these memories: "I cannot say who really supported this establishment. I do know that my grandfather (Sigmund's father) was no longer working, but divided his time between reading the Talmud (in the original) at home, sitting in a coffee house, and walking in the park. Occasionally, he took me with him, when the others were too busy to occupy themselves with me. Tall and broad, with a long beard, he was very kind and gentle, and humorous in the bargain—much more so than my grandmother, whom I really feared, though I admired her stateliness and nice clothes she wore when she went out with her friends. It seems to me, as I look back now, that Freud's father lived somewhat aloof from the others in his family, reading a great deal—German and Hebrew (not Yiddish)—and seeing his own friends away from home. He would come home for meals, but took no real part in the general talk as the others. It was not a pious household, but I do remember one *seder* (Passover feast) at which I, as the youngest at the table, had to make the responses to the reading of the song about the sacrifice of the kid. I was greatly impressed by the way my grandfather recited the ritual, and the fact that he knew it by heart amazed me. I liked, too, to hear the stories he would tell about my mother, who, as eldest daughter, seemed to have been his pet; he held her up to me as an example to follow."

In the house where Sigmund was born was a Czech nurse, known as Nannie, whom he affectionately called "that prehistoric old woman." She was Catholic and would take the young child to Mass, speaking frequently of heaven and hell. So impressed was young Sigmund by this experience that he used to preach mock-sermons when he returned home.

Freud related that as a child he was often told of his mother's delight at the prophecy of an old peasant woman who declared at his birth that a great man had come into the world. He stated in his *Interpretation of Dreams* that such predictions must be quite common: "There are so many hopeful mothers, and so many old women whose influence on this earth is a matter of the past, and who have, therefore, turned to the future." He concluded this narrative with this sentence: "Perhaps this story is the source of my longing to become great."

Sigmund received his early religious education from a liberal Jew named Hammerschlag, who lived in the same building as the family of Josef Breuer. Hammerschlag instilled in Sigmund a love of Bible and later, despite his own difficult financial position, assisted him with small sums of money during the years of study at the university. Freud later wrote: "My early familiarity with the Bible story (at a time almost before I had learned the art of reading) had, as I recognized much later, an enduring effect upon the direction of my interest." Freud punctuated many of his works with scriptural quotations such as the footnote in *The Interpretation of Dreams* in which he quoted the text of Isaiah 29:8 as evidence of one's inner desires being fulfilled in dreams: "It shall even be as when a hungry man dreameth, and behold, he eateth; but he awaketh, and his soul is empty; or as when a thirsty man dreameth, and, behold, he drinketh; but he awaketh, and behold, he is faint, and his soul hath appetite. . . ."

Freud's Hebrew was the Ashkenazic pronunciation, East European as opposed to the Spanish or Sephardic. He also learned Yiddish even though Hebrew was the preferred "holy tongue" of his father. In *Psychopathology of Everyday Life,* Freud wrote how he once reproachfully associated himself with the word *hammer,* because of its similarity with the Yiddish form *khamer* (ass).

Despite a knowledge of Scripture, Freud had little acquaintance with subsequent Jewish literary works. In his extensive writings, there was not a single reference to the Talmud, so important to Jewish learning. He did mention Solomon Almoli, the Chassidic mystic, but such references were rare exceptions. Nor could he read the literature in the original. Trude Weiss-Rosmarin in her *Hebrew Moses: An Answer to Sigmund Freud* castigated Freud for his recklessness and impudence in entering into the field of Bible when "he was only a little better posted on ancient Near East history and Bible than the average educated lay person." Others, however, took an opposing view and argued that Freud as a genius was completely tutored in all Jewish studies just as he was knowledgeable in all other fields.

The truth is probably somewhere in the middle. Freud was certainly no Jewish academician. At one time he could not identify the Menorah (the seven-branched candlestick of the synagogue), even though most kindergarten students in a Jewish religious school could probably explain it without difficulty. In a letter to Roback, Freud admitted: "I had such a non-

Jewish upbringing that today I am not able to read your dedication which is evidently in Hebrew letters. In later years I have often regretted this gap in my education." At the same time the research for his works, *The Moses of Michelangelo,* and *Moses and Monotheism,* helped to render a far superior comprehension of his historical antecedents than that attained by the average Jew.

An interesting insight into Freud's early education is gleaned from a letter written to his wife in September, 1909, while he was away participating in a celebration at Clark University. Explaining why he was not Orthodox, he wrote: "My youth happened in a period when our free-minded teachers of religion placed no value on their pupil's acquisition of knowledge in the Hebrew language and literature. This part of my education was therefore quite neglected, which I often regretted later." Brill added his opinion: "Judging by what I know of the Austrian Jews, I can say that any Jewish boy whose Hebrew education was not stressed could not have been brought up very religiously."

1857 When Sigmund Freud was a year old, a government decree prohibited the establishment of Jewish congregations in the province of Lower Austria. Hermann Wagener wrote his *State Encyclopedia* and *The Jew and the State* expressing strong opposition to the granting of political rights to Jews.

1858 Legislation was enacted in Austria restricting the appointment of Jews to civil positions.

It was in this year that Nannie, Sigmund's Czech

nurse, was dismissed for theft. He, however, did not learn the reason for her being discharged until he was 46 years old. Father Dempsey, a noted psychologist, posed the hypothesis that Freud later had a repressed desire to turn Catholic which could be traced back to the infantile fixation to his second mother, Nannie: "Indeed haven't all boys in the middle classes had two mothers, one to respect and one to boss and play with." Some writers have attributed Freud's negative attitude toward religion to the circumstance of losing Nannie at a tender age. Ernest Jones offered this rebuttal: "Yet we have been asked to believe that this precocious two-year old himself divined that it was the result of her sinning against the ethics of her religion and deduced from this that Christianity was a hypocritical mockery. There is no limit to the fantastic whimsies writers will invent to further some adverse criticism of Freud."

1859 Napoleon III's intervention in Italy in the war of 1859 forced Austria to give up Lombardy and recognize the new kingdom of Italy. After the unsuccessful conclusion of the Italian war, a more liberal policy was maintained. Jews were permitted to acquire property and Jewish journeymen were permitted to qualify as master artisans. Clerical party leaders protested this move by declaring that any recognition of Jewish rights would create a menace to the Catholic Church. The Shoemakers' Corporation of Vienna seized the opportunity to insist that Jews be relegated to an inferior level of political, civil and economic rights. The *Centrum* or Catholic party continued the protestations against Jewish rights. In Germany, no close alliance existed between the Roman Church and the anti-Semites, but in Austria, as in France, the attack upon the influence of the Jews found solid support among Catholics, both lay and clergy.

Economic conditions in Freiberg were especially poor during the end of the 1850's. Business difficulties beset the town, as evidenced by the fact that the Vienna train no longer stopped at Freiberg. And as is usually the case, when a country is in the "red," the outlook for minorities becomes "black." The Czechs, frustrated by a desire for independence, found a convenient scapegoat in the Jews—a people who could not even speak their language.

Jewish merchants, such as Jakob Freud, were held responsible for the unhappy situation of inflation, unemployment and abortive nationalistic aspirations. Seeking a better life, the Freuds moved to Vienna and settled in the Pfeffergasse, a small street in the predominantly Jewish quarter called Leopoldstadt. At an early age Sigmund was experiencing the pangs of emigration, which had ever been the lot of his Jewish ancestry.

Vienna, the new home of the Freuds, was the capital of the Austrian Republic. The fabled Vienna on the Danube, at the intersection of vital European trade roads, linked the North to the South and the East to the West. "This geographical situation," declared the *Encyclopedia Americana,* "greatly contributed to make Vienna one of the most important urban centers on the European continent. It has been called frequently—the Paris on the Danube."

No doubt the writer of this description, "the Paris on the Danube," never lived in Leopoldstadt. Freud's son, Martin, subsequently gave a slightly different portrayal of the Vienna of this period: "The removal from the pretty Moravian town of Freiberg with its rural surroundings to the far from clean and overcrowded Jewish quarter of Vienna, the Leopoldstadt, was, after the first excitement of the change, something of a shock to the little boy. The Jews who lived in the Leopoldstadt were not of the best type. A popular song in Vienna which contained the passage 'When the Jews were crossing the Red Sea, all the coffee-houses in Leopoldstadt were empty' suggests where they spent much of their time. But rents were low in this district and my father's family circumstances were poor."

Anti-Semitism in Vienna was ubiquitous just as in Freiberg. The texture of slander woven by the Church as well as the laity formed a mournful chapter in Jewish history. Unscrupulous assaults against Jews were commonplace. And yet, the Jewish population in Vienna continued to grow from 3,739 in 1846, to 9,731 in 1850, and more than 14,000 in 1854. There were pitifully few other places that would tolerate Jews.

1861 Professor Christian Lassen of Bonn wrote a book *The History of Old India* in which he contrasted the ethical character of the Semites with the Aryans: "Civilization has been the gift of but a few nations. Of other races only Egyptians and Chinese, and of the Caucasian only Semites and Aryans have built up human civilization. History proves that Semites do not possess the harmony of psychical forces which distinguishes the Aryans. The Semite is selfish and exclusive. He possesses a sharp intellect which enables him to make use of the opportunities created by others, as we find it in the history of the Phoenicians and, later on, of the Arabs.''

1862 Joseph Ernest Renan, eminent French historian, philosopher and dramatist, in his essays, *Studies of Religious History,* claimed that the Aryans were the fountain-heads of all the great military, political and intellectual movements in the world's history. Semites could only be credited with religious movements. (Notice the increasing uses of the word Semite as opposed to Aryan.)

1865 Sigmund passed an examination to attend Sperl Gymnasium, a year earlier than the usual age of 11 years. For the next six of the eight year course, he stood at the head of his class.

1866 With the appointment of Bismarck as Prussian Prime Minister, the struggle for German unification entered its final stage. Finally, it was settled by ''blood and iron'' in the war of 1866. Austria, supported by the southern German states in this struggle, fought against Prussia's ally, Italy, on land and on sea. Austria's main army was defeated at Sadowa while the Prussian Army advanced to the gates of Vienna. Austria ceded Venetia to Italy and resigned from German affairs. With military defeat came financial bankruptcy and even greater anti-Jewish feelings.

A personal event was to occur at this time which

Freud later recounted in his *Interpretation of Dreams:* "I might have been ten or twelve years old when my father began to take me with him on his walks, and in his conversation, he revealed his views on the things of this world. Thus it was that he once told me the following incident, in order to show me that I had been born into happier times than he: 'When I was a young man, I was walking one Saturday along the street in the village where you were born. I was well-dressed, with a new fur cap on my head. Up comes a Christian, who knocks my cap into the mud, and shouts, "Jew, get off the pavement!" ' " To the boy's question, "And what did you do?" Jakob calmly replied, "I went into the street and picked up the cap." The grown Sigmund Freud later recalled "that did not seem heroic on the part of the big, strong man who was leading me, a little fellow, by the hand. I contrasted this situation, which did not please me, with another, more in harmony with my sentiments—the scene in which Hannibal's father . . . made his son swear before the household altar to take vengeance on the Romans."

The incident impressed Sigmund so profoundly that he identified with Hannibal who, unlike his own father, met insult with heroism rather than expediency or cowardice. It was a goal-oriented identification growing out of Freud's frustration and anxiety. He wanted to model himself after the person who had achieved such lofty goals. Besides swearing undying hatred for Rome, this great Carthaginian leader was of Semitic stock. Many years later, Freud further explained his boyhood hero worship: "Hannibal . . . had been my favorite hero during my years at the Gymnasium; like so many boys of my age, I bestowed my sympathies in the Punic War not on the Romans, but on the Carthaginians. Moreover, when I finally came to realize the consequences of belonging to an alien race and was forced by the anti-Semitic feeling among my classmates to take a definite stand, the figure of the Semitic commander assumed still greater proportions in my imagination. Hannibal and Rome symbolized, in my youthful eyes, the struggle between the tenacity of the Jews and the organization of the Catholic Church . . . I think I can trace my enthusiasm for the Carthaginian general still farther back into my childhood, so that it is probably only an instance of an already established emotional relation being transferred to a new vehicle."

In *Psychopathology of Everyday Life,* Freud explained how he could not forgive his father for the lack of courage he had shown toward "the enemies of our people." "How much better," says Schoenwald, "to make one's self a Semitic hero than to have to endure, as his father had, a Christian insult! How much better to have one's father make him swear, as Hannibal's father made him do, that he would take vengeance on the Romans."

Brill reviewed the events in this way: "Despite his conscious rejection of his father's behavior, this episode seemed to have served as a symbol for a large part of his own attitude towards the trials and vicissitudes of life. For many a hooligan tried to push him into the gutter, but he calmly ignored it and always reacted to it with calm composure. He never complained in adversity and accepted his lot with fortitude. It was this quality of his mind which so often reminded me of Spinoza, the great sage, who anticipated so many of Freud's views. Indeed, the essence of Spinoza's philosophy, which was expressed in his dictum: *Humanas actiones non ridere, nec lugere, nec detestare sed intelligere* (Human actions should not be mocked, should not be lamented, nor execrated, but should be understood), could be taken as the source and origin of Freud's whole system."

1867 With the Austrian losses in Germany, Italy, and Hungary, the existing federal system of government began to disappear. Emperor Francis Joseph's coronation introduced a double-headed centralism in the creation of the dual monarchy of Austria-Hungary. A result of this change was the promulgation of the constitution declaring the principle of religious liberty. The charter granted the people far-reaching civil and individual rights with equality of all citizens before the law together with freedom of settlement and occupation. Theoretically Austria was taking its place among the modern constitutional states, but Vienna continued during the rest of the century (when Freud was growing to manhood) to remain a virulently anti-Semitic city.

Meanwhile, Otto von Bismarck was allying himself with the Liberals, the party affiliation of the majority of German Jews.

1869 A literary movement known as "Young Germany" was labeled "Young Palestine" by Wolfgang Menzel, an influential scholarly critic, whose writings frequently stressed the sentiment that everything odious must also be Jewish. The same feeling was expressed in Richard Wagner's pamphlet, *The Jew in Music.* Wagner, the alleged illegitimate son of a Jewish actor, Ludwig Geyer, urged the Church to forsake the Old Testament, "the Bible of those Jews who are responsible for the decadence in culture, art and ethics."

Sigmund was given the collected works of Baruch Löb Börne, the Jew who had converted for the purpose of gaining wider recognition as a world idealist. Later, Börne's essays were to stimulate Freud in formulating the therapeutic method of free association.

1870 Industrial capitalism arrived in Austria at this time. Alfred Adler was born in Vienna on February 7th of Jewish parentage. Later he became the founder of "Individual Psychology."

1871 From 1871 to 1878 the Germans dominated the Austrian government and the ministry of Prince Adolf Wilhelm Auersperg.

The Talmud Jew, a book filled with fabrications and forgeries, exercised a very strong influence and achieved importance. The author was a Roman Catholic priest, Augustus Rohling, of the Rhineland, whose anti-Semitic activities dated from the time he was appointed Professor of Catholic Theology at the University of Prague, then an Austrian provincial university. Rohling "quoted" the Talmud to demonstrate the dangerous, inferior, criminal character of the Jews and charged that the Jews considered it their religious duty to physically extract blood from the bodies of

Christian children. After Rohling's book appeared, the Talmud became a common subject of conversation in cafes, at club meetings and at popular gatherings. "Numberless brochures against the Talmud flooded the book market and were disseminated gratis to the humblest laborer's cottage," reported Rabbi Josef Samuel Bloch of Vienna. Rabbi Bloch accused Rohling of perjury and confronted him with the testimony of other Christian scholars who also declared *The Talmud Jew* an outright forgery.

In Zurich, Hermann von Scharff-Scharffenstein in his *The Unmasking of the Modern Jew* claimed that the wickedness of the Jesuits was due to the large number of Jews in the order. Even in France, the home of the "Rights of Man," agitation was being directed against the alien character of the Jew.

1872 Friedrich von Hellwald said in the Austrian weekly *Ausland:* "The Jews are not merely a different religious community but—and this is to us the most important factor—ethnically an altogether different race. The European feels instinctively that the Jew is a stranger who immigrated from Asia. The so-called prejudice is a natural sentiment. Civilization will overcome the antipathy against the Israelite who merely professes another religion, but never against the racially different Jew. The Jew is cosmopolitan, and possesses a certain astuteness which makes him the master of the honest Aryan. In Eastern Europe, the Jew is the cancer slowly eating into the flesh of the other nations. Exploitation of the people is his only aim. Selfishness and lack of personal courage are his chief characteristics; self-sacrifice and patriotism are altogether foreign to him."

In the Reichstag Bishop von Ketteler of Mayence, one of the founders of the *Centrum,* the Catholic party, mocked Ludwig Bamberger, a Jewish deputy to Parliament.

1873 Sigmund graduated from the Gymnasium and had to make a decision regarding his future career. Childhood dreams of someday becoming a great general or minister of state vanished in the face of reality. The reality was that Freud was a Jew and in Jones' words: "For a Viennese Jew the choice lay between industry or business, law and medicine." Sigmund entered the University of Vienna to study medicine at the age of 17.

Burgeoning financial and industrial activity was partly annihilated by the great crash of 1873 from which Austria recovered painfully and slowly. The serious financial crisis produced an ill-feeling against the stock exchange and subsequently against liberalism and the Jews. There were sharp attacks on the "Jewish cosmopolitan financiers" by the Christian Socialists. As anti-Semitism increased, the *Israelitische Allianz* in Vienna was founded with a similar program as the *Alliance Israelite Universelle.* Their purpose was to aid the Jews of Galicia in the struggle for survival by providing schooling and preparatory courses for careers in farming.

1875 The Freud family moved to a large abode in the Jewish quarter of Leopoldstadt at Kaiser Josef-strasse. Sigmund made his first visit to England to see his half-brother, Emmanuel. Ernest Jones called England "the land of Sigmund's dreams"—where one could bring up one's children far from the daily persecutions that Jews were subject to in Austria. The visit heightened Freud's long-standing admiration for Oliver Cromwell, enhanced, no doubt, by Cromwell's welcoming the Jews back into England. So strong was Freud's admiration for Cromwell that he later named his second son after him. During this visit, a talk with his half-brother had the effect of softening the criticism of his father over the "cap-in-the-gutter episode." Freud related that he would often indulge in the fantasy of being Emmanuel's son and thus was he spared the anti-Semitism of Vienna.

In a similar vein, Fritz Wittels in his biography noted: "In Austria, Freud had never been able to escape the sense of inferiority which early affected him, as it does all Jews in German-speaking lands, and especially those who move in intellectual circles. In England, Freud renewed acquaintance with members of his family who had escaped this danger."

1876 Freud graduated from the medical school of the University of Vienna. From 1876–1882, he studied physiology at the General Hospital under Professor Ernst Brücke. Two years earlier, Dr. Brücke's *Lectures on Physiology* set forth the radical theory that the laws of physics and chemistry applied to the dynamic living organic system. Freud published his first original work, 86 pages concerning the recondite testes of the eel.

1878 On May 11th, Hödel, a vagabond, made an attempt upon the life of Emperor William I, the German Emperor and Prussian King. In retaliation for Hödel's political leanings, the government introduced a bill in the Reichstag against socialistic agitations. This bill was rejected. However, there was wide-spread sympathy for the monarch. Jews, who were considered liberal, were therefore suspected of being anti-Emperor. The government dissolved the Reichstag, and new elections on July 30th brought an increase in conservative members. A *Neuer Wahlverein* (New Electoral Society) formulated a platform proclaiming the necessity for a revision of the liberal legislation of previous years. The aim of the platform was to win the majority of the people over to the unprogressive program of the Christian-Socialist Party (*Christlich-Soziale Partei*). The founder of this movement was the court chaplain, Adolf Stöcker, whose purpose was to provide a release for the political dissatisfaction of the people. Election day, July 30, 1878, is sometimes called the birthday of anti-Semitism although the word itself had not yet been coined.

Francis Palücky, the leader of the Czechs in Austria, said in his farewell speech that all Jews were shylocks.

Theodore Herzl, at the age of 18, moved to Vienna with his parents.

1879 The Taaffe government, the longest-lived cabinet in modern Austria (1879–1893), steered a new course that strengthened the influence of the Church in education. When the Liberals seceded from his ministry, Count Eduard von Taaffe threw his support to the Czechs, Slavs, clericals and reactionaries. Laws were enacted to debar Jews from teaching in country districts.

In Germany, President MacMahon resigned. Even though the Liberals had aided Bismarck in his war against the Catholic Church, the Iron Chancellor took advantage of the exigencies of the time, such as the attempted assassination of William I, to consolidate his position. After leading the onslaught for seven years against the Catholic Party (*the Kulturkampf*), Bismarck suddenly made peace with Rome. The Liberal Era was ended, for his reactionary principles were to leave reverberations in France, Germany and Austria.

Freud had disdain for Bismarck and predicted that the Iron Chancellor's demise would bring universal relief. Many other Jews shared the same sentiment. Some of Freud's analytical friends, however, went beyond the objective political reality. They pointed to the coincidence of Jakob Freud's year of birth being the same as Bismarck's (1815) and hypothesized that Freud really wanted his own father's death.

The expression, anti-Semitism, has been used throughout this book. So far as can be determined, the term was not printed until 1879 when a converted Jew, Wilhelm Marr, became the founder of the Anti-Semitic League. Nevertheless, the existence of anti-Jewish feelings was as old as antiquity, as revealed in the Book of Esther where the charge was made that the Jews were a "people scattered abroad and dispersed among the people in all the provinces of thy kingdom;

and their laws are diverse from all people; neither keep they the king's laws; therefore it is not for the king's profit to suffer them."

The term, anti-Semitism, had its origin in the ethnological theory that the Jews as Semites were different from the Aryan or Indo-European populations and could never be assimilated with them. The idea of an instinctive racial hostility supplied Jew-haters with a new, attractive catchword derived from the "science" elucidated in the writings of the Frenchman, Count Joseph Arthur de Gobineau in his *Essay on the Inequality of the Human Race.* His "scientific" pronouncement declared that of all races, the family known as "Aryan" was the source of "everything great, noble, and fruitful in the works of man," with the most creative branch of the Aryans being the Germanic. Contrasts between the tall, blond, civilizing Aryan and the short, swarthy, parasitic Semite gave ammunition to generations that would follow. (Aryan is derived from the name Arya, meaning noble.) Writings by Christian Lassen, Ernest Renan and others paved the way with assertions that Jews, because of their racial Semitic characteristics, were greedy, clannish, obstructionist and unpatriotic.

1880 Austria's first definitely anti-Semitic party was formed under the leadership of Reichsrath deputy, Georg Ritter von Schönerer. The party was violently anti-Habsburg and "racially" anti-Jewish. Vienna was the center of the anti-Semitic activity and had as its protagonist the astute lawyer, Karl Lueger. Like Bismarck, he had started his political career with the aid of Jewish friends. Later, Dr. Lueger hoped to win the bourgeois vote in order to defeat the controlling Liberal Party that was supported by the Jews of Vienna. Through his ability as a demagogue, Lueger succeeded in forming the Christian Socialist Party. A number of the clerical high nobility, under the leadership of Prince Liechtenstein, helped him in this task. Meanwhile, Anton von Schmerling, a former minister-president in the Austrian House of Lords, urged the instruction of German in school to overcome the advantageous position of Jewish soldiers who, owing to their knowledge of the German language, had better chances of promotion to the position of non-commissioned officers. He asserted, "Personally, I am not in sympathy with the Jews." In public meetings, not only Stöcker, the founder of the Christian-Socialist Party, but also his adjutants, Förster and Henrici, denounced the Jews as a danger to the nation. In municipal elections, anti-Semitism was made the central issue. Women's associations were formed for the sole purpose of boycotting all Jewish merchants. A plan was formulated to enlist the support of university students.

1881 In the year that Freud received his medical degree from the University of Vienna, anti-Jewish feelings in Eastern Europe were at an all-time peak. After the accession of Alexander III, riots broke out in Kiev and the southern part of the empire. Property of immense value was destroyed. Jews were expelled from several cities and a large number were killed or seriously injured. Similar occurrences took place in

Warsaw where more than 2,000 families were left homeless. Imperial decrees restricted the Jews' right of residence to the towns of the so-called "Pale of Settlement."

As a result of the *pogroms* (the Russian word for disturbances) many thousands fled in frenzied haste to America. Between 1880 and 1914, almost two million Jews came to the United States from Eastern Europe. At the same time, a movement to return to Palestine was gaining momentum in the hope of resettling the new homeland with Jewish agriculturists. The purpose of this new movement, Zionism, was to provide the Jewish people with the sorely-needed security of nationhood and establish a haven of refuge from the persecutions of the day. When it became evident that anti-Semitism was not merely the remnants of pre-emancipation days but had the overt support of a number of European governments, Zionism grew in numbers and intensity. Its program, as defined by Max Nordau in the First Zionist Congress in Basel, had great appeal for the insecure and disenfranchised Jew: "Zionism seeks for the Jewish people a publicly recognized, legally secured home in Palestine. . . ." It was a secure home where the Jew might live unafraid without being forever taunted. For some, Zionism, like Chassidism, was invested with a fervent religious and messianic zeal and was responsible for men like Theodor Lessing remaining within the Jewish fold with a dream and a vision of freedom. Max Eitingon, a colleague of Freud, settled in Palestine in 1933 and organized the Psycho-Analytical Society there. (The psychological significance of the Jew's preoccupation with the land is discussed in detail in P. F. Zelig's article in the *Psychoanalytic Study of Society*—Volume I, 1960.)

1882 Jones notes that this was the year Sigmund saw a "merry maiden peeling an apple. The first glimpse was a fatal one." Her name was Martha Bernays. Five years Sigmund's junior, she came from a family which included scholars and intellectuals renowned in Jewish history. Her grandfather, Isaac Bernays, had been the Chief Rabbi of Hamburg and an archfoe of the Reform Movement. Isaac's son, Michael, renounced his Jewish faith and embraced Christianity in order to become a Professor of German at the University of Munich. Later he rose to a position of honor unprecedented for a man born the son of a Jew; he became the confidant of mad King Ludwig of Bavaria. Another son, Jakob, said *kaddish* (a prayer for the dead) when his brother Michael left the Jewish faith. Even though Jakob was teaching Latin and Greek at the University of Heidelberg, he never converted for the purpose of attaining a full professorship. (Sigmund later came to understand the impasse of a Jew in academic life.) A third brother, Berman—Martha's father—was a merchant and secretary to the Viennese economist, Lorenz von Stein, and a loyal devotee of Judaism. He died suddenly of a heart attack three years before Sigmund met his daughter.

Martha's mother, Emmeline (nee Philipp), adhered to the strict rules of Orthodox Judaism and taught the children to live accordingly. At the beginning of their long engagement, during which they exchanged letters almost daily, Martha never dared to write to Sigmund on the Sabbath. Later, she did write with a pencil in the garden but not in her mother's presence. She fasted on the Day of Atonement despite the fact that Freud, as a doctor, expressed anxiety about her health and feared the abstention from food would weaken her. He tried his utmost to persuade her to abandon customs such as the observance of *kashrut* (dietary laws), which he regarded as "vain beliefs," but did not completely succeed. (After Sigmund died in London, Martha renewed her interest in Jewish customs and holy days.) Their marriage had to be postponed for five years because of financial difficulties. The delay allowed Sigmund time to continue his medical research on nervous diseases.

This year inaugurated an intense Freud-Breuer friendship which extended to 1894. Josef Breuer was born in Vienna in 1842, in the same social milieu as Freud. He was the son of Leopold Breuer, one of the most famous Chassidic religious leaders of his time. In his *curriculum vitae,* Josef told of the great influence his father played in his development. By the age of 26, Breuer had already achieved recognition by discovering co-jointly with Ewald Hering the self-regulatory mechanism of breathing. Between 1880–1882 Josef had been working on what is now considered the classic case of hysteria, "Anna O.," whose real name was Bertha Pappenheim. It was this same Bertha Pappenheim who had translated the Yiddish manuscript of her ancestor, Glueckel von Hameln, and had worked assiduously for Jewish victims of Russian pogroms. She was an undaunted fighter for social and ethical reform based upon Jewish historical tradition.

Significant historical events were taking place that were to affect Freud and his life. Georg von Schönerer renounced the anti-German policy of Count Taaffe. Together with two other members of the Reichsrath, he formed the nucleus of another anti-Semitic party. He brought to the Diet of Lower Austria and into the Reichsrath a petition signed by 22 members to prohibit the immigration of Russian Jews. Additional support was obtained among the students of the University of Vienna, especially from the largest of the student's societies, the German Book Club.

In nearby Hungary, a fourteen-year old girl, Esther Solymosi, disappeared in the village of Tisza-Eszlár at the same time that three Jewish *Schochetim* (ritual slaughterers of animals) were visiting in the village. Jews were accused of this ritual murder just as they had been implicated in the past. Charges of blood accusation or ritual murder were as old as the twelfth century when a four-and-one-half year old boy, William of Norwich, was found dead on Good Friday. There was the imputation that Jews had killed the Christian lad in order to use *his* blood for the preparation of *matzah* (unleavened bread) and to produce the four cups of red wine for the Passover service. In the 30 years from 1882 to 1911, a number of trials were held against the Jews for ritual murder: one in the East (Corfu, Greece, 1891), two in Russia (Blondes, 1900 and Kiev, 1913), one in Hungary (Tisza-Eszlár, 1882), one in Bohemia (Polna, 1899), and two in Germany (Xanten, 1891, and Konitz, 1900).

The disappearance of Esther Solymosi aroused such excitement that the Jewish deputy Morris Wahrmann and the anti-Semitic Victor de Istóczi came to blows in Parliament. In many places riots occurred. Jews were mobbed, wounded, and killed. Seventeen members of the Hungarian House of Deputies made a motion to repeal the act which had emancipated the Jews. Prominent citizens of Vienna formed committees to assist the new Jewish refugees from Russia. The affair of Tisza-Eszlár exercised its influence upon conditions in Austria and reverberations were felt throughout the world.

Leo Pinsker, the Russian-Jewish physician, in his *Auto-Emancipation,* diagnosed the Jewish problem as the tragic illusion of the Jews of Europe to hope for relief from the nations in which they lived. The solution: Palestine—a country which spelled new hope for him and countless others. Colonization now started in the Holy Land with the assistance of Baron Edmond de Rothschild of Paris. The Bilu movement among Russian Jewish students (abbreviation, *Beth Yaakov L'chu V'nelcha:* O House of Jacob let us go) was formed on the premise that life was intolerable for the Jews in Eastern Europe; that migration to any country but Palestine could only perpetuate the old cycle of a wandering, homeless people; and that it was time for the Jews to return to their ancient homeland. Although Sir Moses Montefiore's plan for establishing agricultural settlements in Palestine had virtually been ignored many years before, the new wave of persecutions changed the entire picture. Jewish population in Palestine rose from 12,000 in 1850 to 35,000 in 1882.

It is estimated that 30,000 Jews emigrated to America in this one year alone. Chassidism gained new adherents with its emphasis on the "joy of life" against an environment of hate.

Freud was not unaware of the events affecting the Jewish people. With a friend he discussed the psychiatric diagnosis of the principal witness of the trial in Tisza-Eszlár. He was gratified at the successful outcome of the case, but had little hope that the verdict would diminish the prevailing anti-Semitism.

In a letter of August 26th, Freud expressed amazement at the intimate knowledge of Jewish ways displayed by the non-Jew, George Eliot—ways "that we (Jews) speak of only among ourselves." In *Daniel Deronda,* one of her Jewish characters said: "Our people wandered before they were driven out. They wandered for four thousand years and are still wandering. They wandered back to Palestine but will not stop there. They are forerunners of the world not of a state."

1883 Rabbi Josef Samuel Bloch, who denounced Rohling in a series of articles charging him with ignorance and deliberate falsification, abandoned his rabbinic career for public life. He was elected to the Reichsrath where he served until 1885. However, he could not prevent the passage of a law which required that the principal of every public school belong to the same church attended by the majority of the school children. This ordinance tended to bar the Jews from all teaching positions in the country districts and served to deter Jewish students from entering the normal schools.

1884 Otto Rank was born in Vienna into a lower middle-class Jewish family. At this time, Freud was discovering the anesthetic properties of cocaine. In Vienna, Pattai, a candidate running for election on an anti-Semitic platform, was defeated.

1885 Soon after being appointed *Privatdocent* (Instructor) at the University of Vienna, Freud left for Paris to study with Jean Martin Charcot. This French neurologist had some success with hypnosis, particularly in the treatment of hysteria. The title of *Privatdocent* was given to the more promising young scientists and usually was an advanced step toward a professorship. Freud remained *Privatdocent* for the unusually long period of 12 years.

Freud spent six weeks at Wandsbek in the hope of establishing better relations with Martha's mother. The Bernays were not excited at the prospect of their daughter being married to a non-believer, even though a physician. Martha's brother, Eli, said: "They would have preferred Martha to marry an old Rabbi or *schochet* (ritual slaughterer)."

Eduard von Hartmann in his treatise, *Judaism in the Present and the Future,* insisted that Jews relinquish their natural sense of race and their consciousness of self-solidarity and adapt themselves wholeheartedly to the German culture.

Bloch founded the *Union of Austrian Jews* intended to create a common Jewish spirit and combat anti-Semitism. His aim was "to promote a love for Jewish learning among the Jews of Austria and to further their interests; to oppose and dispel the widespread errors in regard to the Jews and the prejudice against them; and to combat the efforts to increase the severity of the religious and racial opposition to them."

Freud was scorned and derided after he had told one of his fellow physicians that he was neither an Austrian nor a German but a Jew.

1886 Freud returned to Vienna for several reasons. First of all, he resumed his practice of medicine specializing in neuropathology. His mother had written him a letter earnestly beseeching the blessings of God on his new professional endeavors. The date of opening of his private practice was April 25th, Easter Sunday. It has been suggested that this was a curious time to choose since everything was closed on that holy day. "To begin work on such a day seemed like an act of defiance," interpreted Maryse Choisy.

His second purpose for returning to Vienna was to marry Martha. Thoughts of a Jewish wedding service appalled him. After once attending a Jewish ceremony, he wrote a derisive 16 page letter on its spirit of pious mockery. He shrank from this possible travesty to the point where he thought he could not bring himself to stand beneath the traditional *chuppah* (marital canopy) with Martha. Aversion to this Jewish ritual tempted him to consider even the possibility of conversion. He discussed with his friend and partner, Josef Breuer, the possibility of "changing his confession" in order to avoid the ceremony. Breuer said that it was, *"Zu kompliziert"* (Too complicated!) Jones cited the following description: "Freud spent the nights of the 12th and 13th at the house of Uncle Elias Philipp, who was charged with the task of coaching him in the Hebrew *brochos* ((prayers) he would have to recite at the wedding proper that would take place the following day. He probably bit his lip when he stepped under the *chuppah* but everything went off well. Only eight relatives were present besides the immediate family, and the couple then departed for Lübeck.''

Martha was twenty-five and Sigmund, thirty, when they were married and they lived together for 53 years. Commenting on their married life, A. A. Brill wrote: ''Throughout all his trials there was one bright spot, Freud's home life. Those of us who were fortunate enough to be admitted to his home were especially impressed by his placid, nay, ideal family life. A spirit of congeniality and freedom pervaded the atmosphere of his home. It may be trite to state that the master who traced all our good and evil qualities back to early childhood knew how to bring up his children properly. This is not always the case even in the best psychoanalytic families, but in Freud's home one sensed a certain relationship, a sort of subdued freedom, between parents and children, which I have seen nowhere else. Despite the fact that his opponents continually harped on the fact that Freud saw sex in everything, none ever expressed anything against his moral standards. No breath of scandal was ever connected with his name. He brought up three sons and three daughters, of which five are now living.''

Freud's household was not in accordance with traditional Judaism: dietary laws, Sabbath candles, synagogue attendance. There was, however, transmitted the belief that there was something distinctive and fine about being Jewish and that it was desirable to identify with one's co-religionists. The idea of one's Jewishness as a source of energy occurs again and again in Freud's writings. Two limitations were never exceeded by the family; none ever became converted or entered into mixed marriage. The need for companionship with his fellow-Jews always remained with Freud. On February 2nd, he wrote: "Do you know what Breuer said to me one evening? That he had discovered what an infinitely bold and fearless person I concealed behind my mask of shyness. I have always believed that of myself, but never dared to say it to anyone. I have often felt as if I had inherited all the passion of our ancestors when they defended their Temple, as if I could joyfully cast away my life in a great cause."

1887 When Breuer's friendship with Freud started to end, the Fliess period began (1887–1902). Wilhelm Fliess was a Berlin ear, nose, throat specialist who, like Sigmund, was establishing a medical practice and was also interested in the possibilities of framing great biological theories. Once again both colleagues were Jewish and sons of Jewish middle-class business men. Freud subsequently attributed to his younger colleague the discovery of the concept of bi-sexuality.

Two deputies of the French Chamber proposed a law for the expulsion of all Jews from France on the ground that they were exploiting the country and making themselves its masters.

1888 Freud was fascinated at the thought of Rome and repeatedly mentioned the Eternal City in his letters to Fliess. In November, he wrote: "I am not in a state to do anything except the topography of Rome, my longing for which becomes more and more acute."

Seven hundred and eighty-one Jews were baptized in Vienna, and 141 in the other cities of Austria.

1889 Sigmund continued the frequent references to Rome. In February he wrote: "I am curious myself about when Easter in Rome will be possible." Six months later: "What would you think of 10 days in Rome at Easter? . . . I have looked forward to it so long. Learning the eternal laws of life in the eternal city would be no bad combination." This reinforced Father Dempsey's hypothesis of a repressed wish in Freud to turn Catholic. Dempsey said: "We should find in his conscious experience a strong opposing tendency and perhaps a certain ambivalence and in his unconscious the remnant of some infantile experiences of a contrary nature."

Freud was residing in Nancy, France, studying hypnotism under Ambroise-August Liebault and Hippolyte-Marie Bernheim. Anti-Jewish sentiment was so strong in the country of Freud's sojourn that there was established *a National League for anti-Semitism.*

Anti-Semitism was rearing its head in the United States and Canada. Professor Goldwin Smith of Toronto issued charges against the Jews that were characteristic of Germany, Austria and Russia: "tribal exclusivism and parasites."

1890 A law regulated the Jewish population of Vienna and reassessed its taxation. Wretched poverty in Austria-Hungary caused multitudes of Jews to come to America. Approximately 200,000 Jews migrated from Europe to the United States in the years between 1881 and 1890.

1891 Freud published his first book on cerebral paralyses in children, *Hemiplegia of Children and Aphasia.*

On his 35th birthday, his father gave him the Bible which he, Jakob, read as a boy, and inscribed in Hebrew the following:

> "My dear son,
>
> It was in the seventh year of your age that the spirit of God began to move you to learning. I would say the spirit of God speaketh to you: 'Read in My book; there will be opened to thee sources of knowledge and of the intellect.' I have brought it out from its retirement and I send it to you as a token of love from your old father."

This Hebrew inscription replete with metaphors and phrases from the Scriptures demonstrated a sound comprehension of the Hebrew language by the father as well as familiarity with Holy Writ.

Thirteen anti-Semitic members were elected to the Reichsrath. The members were divided into two different groups: Ultra-Nationals, with Schönerer at their head, who were in favor of annexation of the German part of Austria by Pattai; and Clericals, under Prince Liechtenstein and Schneider. The provincial Diets also showed an increased number of anti-Semitic members.

Pamphlets and newspapers breathed a violence equaled only in the literature of the Jacobins during the French Revolution. Bloch, however, was again elected to serve in the Austrian Reichsrath from 1891 to 1897 and there he fought strenuously against three publishers of blood accusations.

As thousands were coming to America, Baron Moritz Hirsch devised a plan to reduce the Jewish population of Russia through an organized emigration of a third of their number who were to be settled as farmers on free land. He arranged to buy some land in the Argentine, where Jews had already emigrated in 1889, and founded the Jewish Colonization Association to organize a mass emigration of European Jews to various parts of the Americas. Hirsch millions also went toward the establishment of Jewish schools in Galicia, a work which met with encouragement from the Austrian Government.

1892 "Free Association" was being discovered between the years 1892–1895 by Freud and Breuer. Cases were recorded that were later published in *Studies in Hysteria.*

1894 Freud wrote a paper *The Defence Neuro-Psychoses,* in which he described the concept of repression to designate the means whereby instinctual drives are controlled.

Toward the end of September, a document reached the French War Ministry revealing that a French officer was selling military secrets to Germany. Suspicion fell on one officer, Captain Alfred Dreyfus, a peripheral, assimilated Jew. He was arrested and the following month was convicted of high treason by a military court, stripped of his rank and deported to the penal settlement of Devil's Island off the coast of

French Guiana. This was more than just another trial but a reflection of the bitter feeling toward the Jew in France. In the denouncement of Dreyfus was echoed the hate whereby anti-Semitism could still influence masses of people even in the so-called "Enlightened Age."

1895 The Dreyfus Affair brought excitement to a dangerous pitch. In Algeria demonstrations led to bloodshed. France literally divided itself into groups of Dreyfusards and anti-Dreyfusards.

Meanwhile, the anti-Semites succeeded in electing a majority to the municipal council of Vienna. Lueger, after the government had twice refused to confirm him, was now made burgomaster. Impoverished classes joined the Christian-Socialist Party and helped them to attain a majority in the Austrian Provincial House of Delegates. The students' corps took a prominent part in the anti-Jewish campaign by violently attacking Jewish students and even driving them out of school. Ironically, the anti-Semitic Karl Lueger received a special Papal benediction. It was this type of Viennese regime with which Hitler became familiar in his adolescence and attracted him to anti-Semitism. Interestingly enough, Lueger himself was a descendant of a Jewess who had converted when confronted with possible death because of her faith.

Even though Freud and Breuer collaborated in the epoch-making *Studies in Hysteria,* Sigmund was not so absorbed that he failed to notice the recent events. To Fliess, he wrote: "Ida will have told you that in the third electoral district the Liberals were beaten by 46 seats to nil, and in the second district by 32 seats to 14. I voted after all. Our district remained Liberal."

Freud at 39 continued his identity with Judaism by joining the B'nai B'rith Lodge in Vienna for "it seemed to me that I was like a man outlawed, shunned by everyone. . . . That you (B'nai B'rith) were Jews only suited me the more, for I myself was a Jew, and it always seemed to me not only shameful but downright senseless to deny it. . . . On Saturday evenings I indulge in an orgy of taroc (cards) and I spend every other Tuesday evening among my Jewish brethren."

Vacations were taken by the Freud family to those areas where there were large numbers of Jews. Martin Freud reminisced: "Until 1895, while we were still growing, our summer plans were not ambitious. Our parents were content with places not more than a two- or three-hour railway journey from Vienna, like those at the foot of the Rax and the Schneeberg, easterly spurs of the Alpine chain. But after 1895, we went farther afield, to the Alt-Aussee, which was not, however, an unusual nor adventurous choice, because many of Vienna's middle-class families, a good proportion of whom were Jewish, went there."

Many Jews were converting to Christianity because of the unfavorable conditions in Austria. At one time, Max Graf expressed doubt concerning the wisdom of raising his infant son as a Jew, for the child had been born in the midst of an anti-Semitic ferment whipped up by the Viennese demagogue. Freud said to him: "If you do not let your son grow up as a Jew, you will deprive him of those sources of energy which cannot be replaced by anything else. He will have to struggle as a

Jew and you ought to develop in him all the energy he will need for the struggle. Do not deprive him of that advantage."

There were many responses to anti-Semitism. Theodor Herzl was aroused by the Jewish hatred in the capitals of Austria and France where, as a correspondent of the Viennese daily, *Neue Freie Presse,* he followed the Dreyfus affair in its early stages. He suddenly realized that anti-Semitism was not merely propagated by ignoramuses: "It was the fate of the minority Jews which rendered them so vulnerable whenever unscrupulous but by no means illiterate demagogues wished to exploit the deep-rooted intolerance for the unlike in the masses." In the early days of May, Herzl addressed a letter to Baron de Hirsch, the German-Jewish philanthropist. The opening paragraph contained the words, "I want to discuss with you a Jewish political plan—the effects of which will perhaps extend to days when you and I are no longer here." Within a few days he outlined this plan in a 65-page pamphlet. It was the first draft of his famous book entitled *The Jewish State.*

To complete the picture, Dreyfus arrived this year at the penal settlement of *Les Iles du Salut.*

1896 Freud's contacts in Vienna were almost exclusively with Jews. His first public lecture on "The Interpretation of Dreams," five years before the appearance of the book, was delivered to the Fraternity of Jewish Students.

Freud began his investigations in the treatment of the bizarre symptoms of the mental disorder of hysteria. With Breuer as co-author, in *Studies in Hysteria,* they observed that the peculiar behavior of a patient made sense in terms of an important episode in her past which she had forgotten. The illness appeared to consist in re-enacting a fragment of the past recoverable under hypnosis. Her specific symptoms were not "accidental."

Jew-haters were triumphant this year as they gained a majority in the Provincial Houses of Lower Austria and became a powerful group in the lower house of the Reichsrath. Lueger was re-elected but was vetoed by the Emperor. In a letter to Fliess in which he discussed his struggle to stop smoking, Freud wrote that he "only overindulged one day for joy at Lueger's non-confirmation in office."

Herzl's treatise *The Jewish State* was published even though he was still undecided as to whether the Argentines or Palestine should be the site of this home of refuge. He wrote: "The Jewish question still exists. It would be foolish to deny it. It was inherited from the Middle Ages, and civilized nations apparently are not able to get rid of it. The Jewish question exists wherever Jews live in appreciable numbers."

In France, Colonel Georges Picquart discovered that Dreyfus was not guilty. The real culprit was Major Esterhazy. A friend of the spy, Colonel Henry, did his best to prevent the exposure of this judicial "murder" for he himself was implicated in the affair, having forged a certain document.

1897 Elections to the Reichsrath brought losses to the Liberals and gains to the anti-Semites, notably the

Christian-Socialists. Weakness of the government, manifested by the frequent changes of ministries, encouraged further riots against the Jews. The populace insisted and after the fifth election, confirmation could no longer be withheld. Lueger was made burgomaster with dire consequences for the Jews. Police regulations of tradesmen and peddlers were manipulated to work to the disadvantage of Jews. In the school administration disabilities were imposed against the Jews.

Discrimination appeared everywhere with pogroms under the bigoted reactionary Nicholas II in February and April. Mob violence was also directed against the Jews in Bucharest in December.

Freud had been a *Privatdocent* for twelve years and was now proposed as *Professor Extraordinary.* He expressed his expectation in a letter to Fliess: "The vote is going to take place any day." The Board of Professors of the medical faculty voted by a majority on June 12, in favor of Freud's being awarded this title of Professor. Yet, he was not appointed, attributable to the anti-Semitic policy of the Ministry of Education.

Freud wrote to his friend, Wilhelm: "I am all the more pleased that you are at work again. We share like the two beggars one of whom allotted himself the province of Posen; you take the biological, I, the psychological. Let me confess that I have recently made a collection of deeply significant Jewish stories." He continued to speak before Jewish groups, such as the B'nai B'rith, where he gave a more elaborate account of his dream theory.

The first Zionist Congress convened in the old Swiss Rhine city of Basel. Dr. Lippe of Jassy, a follower of *Hoveve Zion* (Lovers of Zion), offered this benediction: "The world has always been badly informed about us. The feeling of unity among us, which the world so often and so bitterly throws up to us, was in process of dissolution when the tide of anti-Semitism rose about us. Anti-Semitism has given us our strength again."

1898 Émile Zola, the French novelist, had always been an outspoken opponent of anti-Semitic ideas and wrote articles in opposition to the Jew-baiting Edouard Drumont. Once again he threw himself into the fight for freedom with a plea for the annulment of the verdict against Dreyfus. In *J'Accuse* (I Indict) he wrote: "If you hide the truth under the earth, it gathers there and assumes such explosive force that on the day it bursts, it blows up everything round about." Zola was convicted for defamation of the army and sentenced to one year of prison.

Freud was again by-passed for Professor Extraordinary. How refreshing and unusual then for Freud to learn of a man like Émile Zola who risked his life for the Jew, Dreyfus. In a letter to Fliess, Freud wrote: "Zola keeps us breathless. He is a fine fellow, a man with whom one could get on."

Israelitish, an Austrian Relief Association, was founded to ameliorate the frightful poverty among the Jews of Galicia.

1899 The murder of Agnes Hruza at Polna, Bohemia, caused great excitement with the charge of ritual murder revived again. A Jew named Hülsner was falsely indicted and found guilty by a jury.

A child was born at half past six on the evening of

April 20th in the *Gasthof Zum Pommer,* a modest inn in the town of Braunau am Inn, Austria. He was to leave an imprint on the life of Freud and countless others. Unlike Breuer, Rank, Fliess and Adler, the infant was not of the Jewish faith. His name—Adolf Hitler!

Again Freud expressed his kinship as well as indebtedness to a Jew. This man's name was Josef Popper-Lynkeus. Josef was born in the ghetto at Kolin, Bohemia, 1838, attended Jewish elementary schools, and became well-known as a physicist, engineer, and social philosopher. His book, *Phantasies of a Realist,* contained the thought that distortion in dreams was due to the censorship of unwelcome thoughts. Like Freud, he professed his repudiation of all formal religious creeds, but declared his sincere attachment to the Jewish people. In 1886, he published anonymously *First Bismarck and Anti-Semitism,* attacking the anti-Jewish policies of the German Chancellor and the anti-Semitic writings of Dühring, von Hartmann, and Richard Wagner. Popper eventually became a Zionist and maintained that only the establishment of a Jewish state could dispel anti-Semitism. In his *On the History of the Psychoanalytic Movement,* Freud wrote: "I found the essential characteristic and most significant part of my dream theory—the reduction of dream-distortion to an inner conflict, a kind of inward dishonesty—later in a writer who was familiar with philosophy though not with medicine, the engineer J. Popper." In an essay entitled *My Contact with Josef Popper-Lynkeus,* Freud stated that after he had discovered Popper's treatment of dream-distortion he read all of his works. Freud continued: "A special feeling of sympathy drew me to him, since he too had clearly had painful experience of the bitterness of the life of a Jew and of the hollowness of the ideals of present-day civilization."

1900 Census takers in Vienna reported 146,926 Jews in the city. Five hundred and fifty-nine of these Jews converted to Christianity in this one year alone.

Freud expressed some of his innermost feelings in a book which he considered his masterpiece and the foundation of all psychoanalysis: *The Interpretation of Dreams.* In the preface, he stated: "The Jewish problem is concern about the future of one's children, to whom one cannot give a country of their own, concern about educating them in such a way that they can move freely across frontiers."

All the names proposed for Professor Extraordinary were ratified with the sole exception of Sigmund Freud. In a dream, Freud assumed the role of the fanatic Minister of Education who had bigotedly rejected Sigmund in the bid for a higher position in the University. In the fantasy character of Minister of Education, Freud proceeded to abuse two of his own Jewish colleagues. Kagan analyzed the incident in this way: "In this dream of wish-fullfillment there is self-hate as a Jew. There is also the frustration-aggression pattern. To compensate for his frustrations against a stronger but real enemy, the Jew aggresses against a fellow-Jew, an imaginary but a vulnerable foe."

Freud wrote a letter to his friend Wilhelm stating: "Well, I really am 44 now, a rather shabby old Jew, as you will see for yourself in the summer or autumn."

He explained his prospects of a trip to Rome: "Otherwise Vienna is Vienna, that is to say extremely revolting. If I closed with 'Next Easter in Rome' (at the end of the Passover service, traditional Jews wish each other: 'Next year in Jerusalem'), I should feel like a pious Jew. So until we meet in the summer or autumn, in Berlin or where you will."

1901 On Monday, September 2nd, Sigmund accompanied by his brother Alexander, arrived in Rome. It was the first of seven visits that he was to subsequently make to the Eternal City. Of all the places, it was Rome that Freud yearned to see ever since as a boy he identified with Hannibal, the great Semitic general who, too, had longed to see and conquer this city. (cf., 1866) The interest was more than a fascination with those early traditions from which much of the world's heritage had emerged. In *The Interpretation of Dreams,* Freud called Rome "the Promised Land" which symbolized for him only one thing—"the organization of the Catholic Church." He wrote two sentences in explanation of his craving. "The significance for our emotional life," he said, "which the anti-Semitic movement has since assumed, helped to fix the thoughts and impressions of those earlier days. Thus the desire to go to Rome has in my dream-life become the mask and symbol for a number of warmly-cherished wishes, for whose realization one had to work with the tenacity and singlemindedness of the Punic General, though their fulfillment at times seemed as remote as Hannibal's lifelong wish to enter Rome." When Freud at last did reach Rome, it was Michelangelo's statue of Moses which fascinated and magnetized him.

1902 Martin Freud told of his father's promotion: "In the spring of 1902, an event occurred in father's life which not only increased his earning capacity but also improved his social standing and that of his family. He was made a professor, a gesture long overdue since he had been *Privatdocent* since 1885. The fact that father was a Jew was one reason for the delay; the other was that he was a pioneer in a new field of research looked upon by the leading men in psychiatry and psychology as fantastic, and even indecent. The title of professor now conferred on him did not, however, affect the attitude of the university's leading men; they continued to look down on the now middle-aged Jewish doctor and refused to take him seriously."

The family spent their summer holidays in Bavaria at Thumsee. An incident occurred described by Jones: "On returning from a walk they found their way home, which meant crossing the Thumsee to get to their hotel, barricaded by a noisy crowd who were shouting anti-Semitic slogans at them. Swinging his walking stick Freud unhesitatingly charged into them with an expression on his face that made them give way before him. It was by no means his only experience of the kind. I recall a particularly unpleasant one where he also cowed a hostile group that happened on a train journey from Hamburg to Vienna during his engagement time. Freud could on occasion create a formidable impression with a stern and somewhat scowling glance. The last time when it was displayed, and with success, was when he faced the Nazis in his home in 1938."

On the 28th of September, Freud sent Herzl his book *The Interpretation of Dreams* on the recommendation of another member of the *Neue Freie Presse's* editorial board with the suggestion that Herzl review it. Freud wrote: "But at all events, may I ask you to keep the book as a token of the high esteem in which I—like so many others—have held since many years for the poet and the fighter for the human rights of our People."

In October the initial organization of the Psychological Wednesday Society (changed six years later to Vienna Psychoanalytical Society) was organized.

1903 As two other Jews, Paul Federn and Wilhelm Stekel, commenced the practice of psychoanalysis, Freud emerged from his lonely isolation.

Throughout Europe, these were years of intensive Jew-baiting. In Kishinev, circulars were sent out just before Easter announcing the Church's consent to a pogrom taking place on the first three days of the holy festival. The signal was to be indicated by the ringing of the church bells. Jews who tried to defend themselves were disarmed by the police. Events of unprecedented bestiality occurred throughout the following day as the pogrom continued. Finally the government's troops interceded. Casualties included 45 dead; 86 seriously and 500 slightly wounded; and more than 1,000 houses and shops looted.

1904 One of the best known of Freud's works among the general public, *The Psychopathology of Everyday*

Life, was published. Freud gave an early impression to his concept of religion: "I believe in fact that a great part of the mythological view of the world which reaches far into the most modern religion, is nothing other than psychological processes projected into the outer world. The obscure apprehending of the psychical factors and relations of the unconscious is mirrored—it is hard to put it otherwise; one has to use here the analogy with paranoia—in the construction of a supersensible reality, which science has to retranslate into the psychology of the unconscious. One could venture in this manner to resolve the myths of Paradise, the Fall of Man, of God, of Good and Evil, of Immortality and so on, thus transforming Metaphysics into Metapsychology."

In Vienna, 617 Jews were baptized into Christianity and Theodor Herzl died at the age of 44. Just before his death he had an interview with Goluchowski, the Austrian Foreign Minister. Goluchowski had enthusiastically supported Herzl's Zionist plans and thought that the Great Powers should sponsor them even to the extent of financial support. "Excellency," Herzl suggested, "will you head such an effort?" "This is not the moment. We are not finished in Macedonia," said the Austrian official.

1905 The Russian Revolution had its reverberations in Austria where a faint attempt was made to protect racial minorities. Every Austrian was to vote for national representatives according to the language of his own ethnic group. Accordingly, the Jews of Vienna, who spoke German, would have to cast their ballot for the German-speaking Christian-Socialists, an anti-

Semitic party. Even the occasional reforms in government led to bitter disappointment.

During one of the lectures at the University on the subject of "Dreams and Their Interpretations," Freud alluded to Herzl. Freud, according to E. Simon, recounted how Herzl had once appeared to him in a dream: "An appearance filled with glory, with a dark yet pale countenance, adorned with an attractive black beard, and with eyes which expressed infinite grief. The apparition attempted to persuade Freud of the need of immediate action if the Jewish people were to be saved. These words astonished him by their logic and their pent-up emotion. Sigmund Freud added that he had never set eyes on Herzl, neither had he ever been interested in his ideas. But after the dream he once encountered him in a certain street in a bus traveling to Wahringer Strasse, and was astonished at the resemblance between Herzl's apparition in the dream and his actual appearance."

Wit and Its Relation to the Unconscious was published replete with an uncommon number of Jewish anecdotes. Freud loved the dialectical Jewish joke with its characteristic posture of inferring. In this volume, he cited two kinds of humor. First, the non-sexual Jewish jokes with an emphasis upon social amenities such as food, class distinction, customs, and traditions. Then he reviewed the general Christian stories which possessed a flavor of sexuality. In his theory of the Jewish wit, Freud enumerated these distinctive traits:

1. A sharp *self-criticism* that has emerged from the soul of Jewish national life. "Jews know their real shortcomings as well as their merits, and the interest

of the person himself in the thing to be criticized produces the subjective determination of the wit-work which would otherwise be difficult to bring about. Incidentally, I do not know whether one often finds a people that makes merry so unreservedly over its own shortcomings."

2. A *democratic mode of thought* which is indifferent to class distinctions.

3. An emphasis is placed upon the *social principles* of the Jewish religion.

4. There are the elements of *religious revolt.*

5. A *hapless poverty* is endured by the miserable Jewish masses.

6. The general spiritual atmosphere permeating Jewish wit as one of constant *alertness, distrust,* and *suspicion.*

Brill, in commenting on this book, stated: "If one reads this very profound work, one finds that many of the witticisms which Freud selected as illustrations for his theories are of Jewish origin, and some, if divested of the theoretical material for which they are façades, are far from creditable to the race. This has been noticed by some observers who criticized Freud for having selected these examples. It occurred to me that the author has unconsciously utilized these Jewish jokes to unburden himself of the tension which was accumulated in him since his early childhood by some anti-Semitic experiences."

Three Essays on the Theory of Sexuality, which proclaimed the significance of infantile sexuality in the causes of neurosis, was also published. In a scathing denouncement of Freud's principles of psychoanalysis,

Andrew Salter did admit: "Freud took the obscenity of sex, and made sexuality an object of study. . . . His sexually liberating influence on the post-Victorian world merits strong commendation."

1906 The Supreme Court of Appeal vindicated Dreyfus and restored to him his rank in the army.

Martin Freud told of an American girl, Julia, who was visiting Europe and of her shock and humiliation caused by the manner which customs officials used in their mistreatment of Jews. Freud and his family went to a summer resort in the southerly part of Tyrol near the Italian border. A man introduced himself to Sigmund and after giving his name and title remarked: "*Noi siamo Ebrei*" (We are Jews). Freud said, "So are we." Martin commented: "This may seem an unusual way of introducing oneself, but as I then thought, and still think, it is a practical proceeding which allows everybody to know just where he is."

1907 A resolution for a *Numerus Clausus* (restricting Jewish enrollment in the gymnasia, and other schools) was supported by all the anti-Semitic groups. The resolution was defeated only with the aid of the Slavic parties.

Freud, then 51, published a paper *Obsessive Acts and Religious Practices* in which he traced the correlation of "obsessive acts in neurotics and those religious observances by means of which the faithful give expression to their piety." Resemblances were noted between religion and the compulsive urge to perform fixed ceremonials. In each case the act has the function of supporting the repression of a prohibited need or desire. Since religion is of the same nature as obsessional neurosis, the pathological unhealthy conditions must be treated as quickly as possible by analysis. Freud concluded the work by the reference to the analogies which make one "venture to regard the obsessional neurosis as a pathological counterpart to the formation of a religion, to describe the neurosis as a private religious system and religion as a universal obsessional neurosis."

In the first edition of the *Zeitschrift für Religionpsychologie* (*Journal of the Psychology of Religion*), Freud proclaimed that the sense of compulsion in obsessional neurosis was in essence a sexual temptation, whereas in religion, the compulsions were most concerned with aggressive and anti-social behavior.

Max Eitingon (Eitingon and Hanns Sachs were perhaps the most committed to Judaism) visited Freud. A later visit to Palestine foreshadowed Eitingon's final withdrawal to that country at the first moment of Hitler's ascendancy.

Among the other early guests of the Psychological Wednesday Society was C. G. Jung. Freud was immediately impressed and strongly affected by him. After years of abuse by the outside world, Freud now welcomed his new Swiss adherent, his first foreign one, and not the least important, his first non-Jewish colleague. In the new relationship, Freud was once again caught in a transference situation akin to his involvement with Wilhelm Fliess. Later, when the relationship with Jung began to wane, Freud compared it to a corresponding point in his friendship with Fliess because of the similar experience of uncheerfulness.

1908 Freud was at last being recognized and acclaimed. The First International Psychoanalytical Congress was held in Salzburg. Karl Abraham founded the Berlin Society. Two new disciples, A. A. Brill and Ernest Jones, visited Freud. When Freud's friendship for Jung was intensified, the Jewish members were distressed. Jones believed that their attitude was engendered by a suspicion against all non-Jews with its rarely failing expectation of anti-Semitism. "Freud himself," Jones said, "may have shared this to some extent, but for the time being it was dormant in the pleasure of being at last recognized by the outer world." Karl Abraham was especially wary of Jung. When a criticism was made, Freud defended the non-Jew, Jung, by saying: "We Jews have an easier time, having no mystical elements. Be tolerant. Don't forget it is easier for you to follow my thoughts than for Jung. To begin with you are completely independent and racial relationship brings you closer to my intellectual constitution. Whereas he, being a Christian and the son of a pastor, can only find his way to me against great inner resistances."

Freud was convinced that psychoanalysis was being stifled because of anti-Semitism and the fact that there was an overwhelming number of Jews in the movement. He wrote another letter to Abraham commenting on the anti-Jewish feelings in Switzerland: "In my opinion we have as Jews, if we want to cooperate with other people, to develop a little masochism and be prepared to endure a certain amount of injustice. There is no other way of working together. You may be sure that if my name were Oberhuber, my new ideas would, despite all the other factors, have met with far less resistance. Jung's adherence is therefore all the more valuable. I was almost going to say it was only his emergence on the scene that has removed from psychoanalysis the danger of becoming a Jewish national affair."

1909 In some respects, life was happier for the Freud family. The eldest daughter, Mathilde, was married. Sigmund was invited to the United States to participate in the Clark University celebration. Since he was away for the holidays, Freud sent a *Rosh Hashanah* (Jewish New Year) good wishes telegram to his wife and family in Vienna. In addition, Freud had a Christian to lead his movement.

Even a Protestant clergyman, Rev. Oskar Pfister of Zurich, admired Freud's philosophy. Freud was delighted and wrote to his new disciple: "In itself psychoanalysis is neither religious nor the opposite but an impartial instrument which can serve the clergy as well as the laity when it is used only to free suffering people. I have been very struck at realizing how I had never thought of the extraordinary help the psychoanalytic method can be in pastoral work, probably because wicked heretics like myself are far away from that circle." In the same letter Freud suggested that because most people were no longer religious and could not endure their suffering, they had to turn to psychoanalysis to master their "obdurate instinct." Freud even admired proper religious sublimation but added that any success would depend on the maturity of the interpersonal relationship of pastor and parishioner. "You (referring to Pfister) are in the fortunate position of leading them to God and reconstructing the conditions of earlier times, fortunate at least in the one respect that religious piety stifles neuroses."

However, in a case history of Schreber, Freud stated that God was a father-substitute. Schreber's delusional system was characterized by his ambivalent attitude toward God and by his ideas of being emasculated. Freud interpreted this as an attempt by Schreber to overcome his father complex, especially its passive-homosexual component. By means of denial and projection, Schreber protected himself from his homosexual tendencies. "I do not love him, I hate him," the ego first says in self-defense, and according to Freud the projection turns "I hate him" into "He hates me." In this way his own hatred is rationalized into "I hate him because he persecutes me." Persecution represents the homosexual temptation turned into a fearful threat. Destruction of the function of reality testing gives this unsuccessful defense against homosexual temptation its delusional character. The form and content of the delusion show all the features of magical and archaic ego levels. In a postscript to his paper, *Psychoanalytic Notes Upon An Autobiographical Account of a Case of Paranoia,* Freud noted the identity of the psychotic symbols with mythological and religious emblems.

1910 The International Psychoanalytic Association was founded. A leader had to be selected. Freud portrayed Jung as the Swiss knight who would ride forth in shining intellectual armor and carry the cause of psychoanalysis before a world that would not listen to a Viennese Jew. Jung was nominated by Freud for the editorship of the Yearbook and the presidency of the International Psychoanalytic Association. So intent was Freud on having a Christian at the head of his movement that he did not even pause to notice that Jung was not really interested in organizational and administrative duties. The extravagant way that Freud pinned his hopes on Jung, as though he were deliberately raising another person and dismissing himself from the field, was fraught with many overtones. It was an action that was quite out of place, wrote Dr. Ira Progoff, since Freud himself and no one else was the only possible leader for the movement that carried his name. Subsequent events conclusively proved this to be the case. Freud was caught in the fantasy of having someone carry his message to the world—a gallant protagonist speaking in the name of science beyond the reach of anti-Semitic prejudice.

When a protest was voiced on the selection, Freud appeared on the scene and said: "Most of you are Jews, and therefore you are incompetent to win friends for the new teaching. Jews must be content with the modest role of preparing the ground. It is absolutely essential that I should form ties in the world of general science. I am getting on in years, and am weary of being perpetually attacked. We are all in danger." Seizing his coat by the lapels, he said, "They won't even leave me a coat to my back. The Swiss will save us—will save me, and all of you as well."

Freud wrote to Ferenczi of the unfavorable reaction to his theory of anal eroticism: "There one hears just the argument I tried to avoid by making Zurich the center. Viennese sensuality is not to be found anywhere else! Between the lines you can read further that we Viennese are not only swine but also Jews. But that does not appear in print."

In his work *Leonardo da Vinci,* Freud claimed that the Jewish practice of circumcision was the deepest source of anti-Semitism. Freud considered this to be a primeval custom used as a symbolic substitute for castration and an expression of subjection to the father's will. He also stated: "Psychoanalysis has made us aware of the intimate connection between the father complex and the belief in God and has taught us that the personal God is psychologically nothing more than a magnified father. It shows us every day how young people can lose their religious faith as soon as the father's authority collapses. We thus recognize the root of religious need as lying in the parental complex."

In July, he wrote Pfister of his "unbounded admiration and gratitude toward the man who was a true Christian."

Official religious census counts of the population in Austria in 1910 revealed that 90 per cent of the population belonged to the Roman Catholic Church, 4.6 were Jews, 2.33 were Greek Catholics, 2.6 were Protestants, and 0.19 were of other faiths. In Hungary 52.1 per cent were Roman Catholics, 19. were Protestants, 9.7 were Greek Catholics, and 4.5 were Jews.

As a result of persecutions in Russia and Europe, the Jewish population in the United States increased from 50,000 in 1850 to nearly two million in 1910.

Hitler was living in Vienna at this time. Strolling through the Jewish ghettos called the "Inner City," he encountered an alien-looking bearded man with *kaftan* (long coat) and black sideburns. "Is this a Jew?" he asked of himself. He wrote in his *Mein Kampf* of "relieving his doubts by books," and reading the anti-Semitic literature which was in abundance in the "Paris of the Danube." "Gradually," he related, "I began to hate them. I ceased to be a weak-kneed cosmopolitan, and became an anti-Semite." In the spring he left Vienna for Germany because, "My inner revulsion toward the Habsburg State steadily grew . . . Jews and more Jews."

1913 Martin Freud described the conditions of that time: "Anti-Semitic shouts could be heard in the battle between German-Austrian students and their Jewish colleagues. What seemed remarkable to me was that the Jews were fighting back, and fiercely too. This seemed to me out of character and possibly the first time in 2,000 years that Jews, accustomed to being beaten up and persecuted, had decided to stand up for themselves. I felt I was witnessing an historic occasion."

Martin was hurt in a brawl between German-Austrian and Jewish students. In his words: "I had no opportunity to fight these incipient Nazis under equal conditions man to man. I had to content myself with joining in brawls when Jews were outnumbered by five to one, or even more. As I said earlier, I was wounded in such a brawl by a knife-thrust, and as I was the son of a university professor, the newspapers reported the incident with a wealth of detail. I remember when I got home that night, neatly and expertly bandaged, the family were at dinner with a guest, the Reverend Oskar Pfister from Zurich. I apologized for my appearance and father threw me a sympathetic glance. The clergyman, however, got up and approached me to shake hands warmly, congratulating me on being wounded in so just and noble a cause. This sympathy and kindliness from a dignified leader of the Christian Church heartened me considerably, making me feel less like a battered ruffian."

Martin told of his Zionist leanings: "The idea that Jews might abandon meekness as a defence against humiliating attacks was new and attractive to me. A few evenings after the university battle, I went to the headquarters of the Jewish corporation whose members had taken part in it. There were a number of such corporations, but the one I approached, the *Kadimah,* was the oldest. . . . The word *kadimah* meant both forwards and eastwards. The members of the *Kadimah* were Zionists."

Alphonse Maeder had written to Sandor Ferenczi that the scientific differences between the Viennese and the Swiss resulted from the former being Jews and the latter, Aryans. Freud in a letter advised Ferenczi to answer on the following lines. "Certainly there are great differences between the Jewish and the Aryan spirit. We can observe that every day. Hence there would assuredly be here and there differences in outlook on life and art. But there should not be such a thing as Aryan or Jewish science. Results in science must be identical, though the presentation of them may vary. If these differences mirror themselves in the apprehension of objective relationships in science there must be something wrong.''

In October, the final break occurred between Jung and Freud. The two men were never to meet again. It had taken six years for Freud and Jung to come to the parting of the ways. Many years later (about 1935), Jung contrasted Freud's inferior ''Jewish'' psychology with Hitler's perfect scientific doctrines of Aryan superiority. No doubt, the years had changed Jung. But Freud's disenchantment was not only with his Christian disciple. He claimed that his own Jewish colleagues as well had problems with envy and father rivalry.

Jones wrote of the feeling of the Jewish members: ''I became, of course, aware somewhat to my astonishment of how extraordinarily suspicious Jews could be of the faintest sign of anti-Semitism and of how many remarks or actions could be interpreted in that sense. The members most sensitive were Ferenczi and Sachs; Abraham and Rank were less so. Freud himself was pretty sensitive in this respect. He must have wondered how the only foreigner—the only one, for instance, whose mother tongue was not German—would intermingle with a group otherwise so compact, but (referring to Rank) he reassured me: 'You may guess what pleasure it gives me to see your friendly relationship to him, to Ferenczi and the other members of the Committee you yourself founded.' "

Freud wrote an introduction to Rev. Oskar Pfister's book, *The Psychoanalytic Method* of a relationship between psychoanalysis and education and religion: "The question presents itself whether one may not utilize psychoanalysis for the purposes of education as the hypnotic suggestion has been utilized in its time. The advantages of this use of psychoanalysis would be obvious. The educator is prepared on the one hand, through his knowledge of the general human dispositions of childhood, to guess which of the childish dispositions threaten to attain an undesired outlet. If psychoanalysis is of influence in such errors of development, he can bring it into use before the signs of an unfavorable development are established. Thus, he can influence children who are still healthy, prophylactically, by means of the analysis. On the other hand, he can detect the first signs of a development toward a neurosis or perversion and guard the child against such further development, at a time when, for a number of reasons, it would never be taken to a physician. One could conceive that such a psychoanalytic activity on the part of the educator—and the pastor in Protestant countries who occupies a similar position—might afford invaluable assistance and often render the intervention of the physician superfluous. May the application of psychoanalysis in the service of education soon fulfill the hopes which educators and physicians attach to it! A book like this of Pfister's, which will make the analysis known to educators, will then be assured of the gratitude of future generations."

In a monograph, *Totem and Taboo,* Freud, like Jung, began to concentrate upon the behavior of primitive peoples. Freud attempted to understand the phenomenon of totemic religion in relationship to morality and the beginnings of civilization. First he explained the meaning of totem. "As a rule it is an animal, either edible and harmless, or dangerous and feared; more rarely the totem is a plant or a force of nature (rain, water), which stands in a peculiar relation to the whole clan." Then he delved into his main thesis of how religion, civilization and morality had their origin in a primal crime.

Originally, Freud believed that everyone dwelt in primal hordes dominated by tyrannical men who possessed clans of females. As soon as the sons posed a threat to the dominant male who enjoyed exclusive sexual possession of all the women, the boys were driven away by the fear of paternal retaliation. "One day, however, the sons came together to overwhelm, kill, and devour their father, who had been their enemy and ideal." The exiled sons formed a clan motivated by the ambivalent feelings of love and desire to emulate him; and hatred, for they too wanted sexual possession of the women. Simultaneously, the sons could do away with and identify with an object in one way—consuming it.

The primal crime was a cannibalistic murder of the original father. Though the father was now no longer physically present (he was dead), he was psychically present. Through the mechanism of denial, the sons attempted to repress the conscious memory of their deed. Each brother felt an especially intense regret and fear since each one now posed a threat to the other. Would each brother now kill the other to gain the desired females? New rules had to be made. Laws were enacted that members of the same totem (tribes were divided into septs or clans, each taking the name of a totem animal, etc.) were not allowed to enter into sexual relations or marry one another. Thus the taboo against incest and the demand for exogamous marriage. The totem animal was sacrificed for the original human victim, the father. Morality and civilization were beginning.

The hypothesis continued: After a time the totem was no longer a substitute for the primal father who had been both "feared and hated, honoured and envied." Because of a lasting unconscious sense of guilt, the sons attempted to repent for their crime against the ancient father by magnifying him above all else. The father became "the prototype of God himself." The God of modern religion was derived from his animal predecessor and, like the latter, was the object of the individual's love, hatred and guilt feelings. "The psychoanalysis of individual human beings," Freud said, "teaches us with quite special insistence that the god of each is found in the likeness of his father, that his personal relation to God depends on his relation to his father in the flesh and oscillates and changes along with that relation, and that at bottom God is nothing other than an exalted father." Freud concluded: "Totemism, with its worship of a father substitute, the ambivalency toward the father which is evidenced by the totem feast, the institution of remembrance festivals and of laws, the breaking of which is punished by death—this totemism, I conclude, may be regarded as the earliest appearance of religion in the history of mankind, and it illustrates the close connection existing from the very beginning of time between social institutions and moral obligations."

Though Freud wrote as a psychologist, other social scientists studied his findings. Said A. L. Kroeber in his *Anthropology:* "The theory of the primal horde is a so-so story. The psychoanalytic explanation of culture is intuitive, dogmatic and wholly unhistorical." Malinowski, a supporter of psychoanalysis, after investigating the Trobriand Islanders of Melanesia, admitted: "We have found that there is in reality a complete absence of motive for a parricidal crime." Even among the most ardent disciples, the theories of *Totem and Taboo* were subject to criticism and censure.

1914 With the outbreak of war, Austria reverted to an absolutistic system of government. The "dictatorship" article 14 of the Constitution served as legal justification. Within the past 34 years, almost two million Jews emigrated to the United States from Eastern Europe, while the number of Jews in Palestine rose to 85,000.

In March, Freud wrote *The History of the Psychoanalytical Movement* and in August, Jung resigned as president of the International Association. Freud's "Moses of Michelangelo" was published anonymously in the periodical *Imago.* Why anonymously? Freud confided, "Why disgrace Moses by putting my name to it? It is a joke, but perhaps not a bad one." The essay was written at the time when the bridge to the Gentile world, C. G. Jung, had just defected from orthodox psychoanalysis. Jones declared: "This essay is of special interest to students of Freud's personality. The fact alone that this statue moved him more deeply than any other of the many works of art with which he was familiar gives his essay on it a peculiar significance." Freud himself wrote: "For no piece of statuary has ever made a stronger impression on me than this. How often have I mounted the steep steps of the unlovely Corso Cavour to the lonely place where the deserted church stands, and have essayed to support the angry scorn of the hero's glance! Sometimes I have crept cautiously out of the half-gloom of the interior, as though I myself belonged to the mob upon whom his eye is turned—the mob which can hold fast no conviction, which has neither faith nor patience, and which rejoices when it has regained its illusory idols. But why do I call this statue inscrutable? There is not the slightest doubt that it represents Moses, the Lawgiver of the Jews, holding the Tables of the Ten Commandments. That much is certain, but that is all. . . ."

Hanns Sachs commented on the article: "It is as if Freud walked intuitively and unknowingly in the footsteps of his ancestors, and followed one of the oldest Jewish traditions; this is the belief that all Jews, born and unborn alike, were present on Mount Sinai and have there taken upon themselves the yoke of the Law."

Erich Fromm discussed the article in this vein: "Why did Freud write this paper, in which he does not use the psychoanalytic method, and why did he have to hide behind this anonymity, when it would have been quite feasible to publish the paper with a remark that since it was Freud's, it was published even though it was not strictly psychoanalytic? The answer to both questions must lie in the fact that the Moses figure was of great emotional importance to Freud, yet an importance which was not clearly recognized consciously, and against the recognition of which must have existed a considerable resistance."

1915 Anti-Semitic agitation limited the number of Jews admitted to the Vienna bar and prevented refugee Jewish lawyers from practicing in Western Austria.

Freud published *Twelve Essays on Metapsychology.* He was sorely disappointed for he did not receive the Nobel Prize as he had hoped, but understood the reasons: "It would be ridiculous to expect a sign of recognition when one has seven-eighths of the world against one."

Martin Freud described his experience in the Austrian Army with the anti-Semitism that prevailed: "Having been found fit for military service, I had to serve a year with the Austrian Army. Students were let off with a single year in contrast to the three years others less fortunate had to serve with the colours. One day the Colonel, armed with a visiting card brought to him by an orderly, went to the ante-room, which was his habit, to look over the caller as a preliminary move before leading him to his sanctum which he shared with my two friends. He returned alone in some excitement to say, 'Listen, my lads! Let this be a lesson to you! The fellow who sent in his card was a Jew. He wanted to see me. Well, I expect you can guess what happened. I threw him out.' Then, raising his voice, the old fellow went on, 'So long as I am in command here, no Jew will ever enter this room.' Both my friends were Jews, and highly amused Jews at the moment, even tactful Jews who succeeded in hiding their grins."

Sigmund Freud gave university lectures for the last time. He published the clinical paper, *The Transformation of Instincts, with Special Reference to Anal Eroticism,* and described a type of submissiveness found in some forms of hero worship that is based on the unconscious fantasy of being a part of the hero. Devotion to God is correlated with the belief that God without oneself would be as incomplete as oneself without God. Whereas one is actually dependent on the partner, the partner in turn is thought to be magically dependent on oneself.

Professor Franz van Luschan of Berlin called psychiatry "such absolute nonsense that it should be countered ruthlessly with an iron broom. In the Great Times in which we live such old wives' psychiatry is doubly repulsive." Freud responded: "No matter! An old Jew is tougher than a Royal Prussian Teuton."

1917 At first, Freud enthusiastically supported the German side. As the war progressed, he became depressed over the "unworthiness of human beings."

Talk of death prompted him to write the essays (unpublished until after his death) on *Mourning and Melancholia* and *Thoughts for the Times on War and Death.* He wrote to a friend. "The only cheerful news is the capture of Jerusalem by the English and the experiment they propose about a home for the Jews."

During the course of the year, the Allied forces defeated the Turkish armies and occupied the whole territory comprising Palestine. British troops formed the majority of the Army but French and Italian units were included with a special Jewish legion founded by Vladimir Jabotinsky. After a decision of the War Cabinet, the British Government published the policy statement which became known as the Balfour Declaration. It took the form of a letter from Mr. Balfour, then Secretary of State for Foreign Affairs, to Lord Rothschild, whom Dr. Chaim Weizmann had suggested as the addressee. The text read: "His Majesty's Government views with favor the establishment in Palestine of a National Home for the Jewish people, and will use their best endeavors to facilitate the achievement of this object, it being clearly understood that nothing shall be done which may prejudice the civil and religious rights of existing non-Jewish communities in Palestine, or the rights and political status enjoyed by Jews in any other country."

1918 Collapse of the dual monarchy began when Bulgaria withdrew from the war in the last days of September and placed Austria-Hungary open to Allied invasion. Austria-Hungary followed the German example and sued for an armistice on the basis of the

Fourteen Points. The fall of the Habsburgs and the disintegration of the Austro-Hungarian Empire had far-reaching consequences for the capital city. Instead of being the metropolis of an empire of 50 millions, Vienna now became the capital of a small European country with a population of only 6½ millions. Political and economic collapse followed. The city could not support the enormous burden of an army and an administrative organization suitable for a great power but now based upon a huge hinterland that no longer existed. More than 90% of the Jewish population of approximately 200,000 lived in the capital Vienna, and were the most affected by the cut-back of the country's vital arteries.

Subsequent years brought a succession of economic crises, hunger riots, attempts at revolution and frequent national bankruptcy to Austria. With inflation, unemployment, and the frustrated Pan-German dreams, the Jew became once again fair game for the anti-Semitic political parties. Chief Rabbi Hirsch Perez Chajes came to Vienna at this time and tried to rekindle a Jewish pride by a reorganization of the religious community and by making Vienna the focal point for training Hebrew teachers for Eastern Europe and Palestine.

In March and April, the Ukraine declared its independence and the "independent" citizens killed the Jews. Subsequent fighting between the Bolsheviks and the Ukrainian separatists ultimately led to the worst riots that had taken place since the seventeenth century. Between December, 1918 and April, 1921, 1,236 pogroms resulted with 60,000 Jews being killed and more than 70,000 being wounded.

Freud, now 62, wrote to Oskar Pfister on October 9th: "From a therapeutic point of view I can only envy your opportunity of bringing about sublimation into religion. But the beauty of religion assuredly has no place in psychoanalysis. Naturally our paths in therapy diverge here, and it can stay at that. Quite by the way, how comes it that none of the godly ever devised psychoanalysis and that one had to wait for a godless Jew?"

Pfister replied 20 days later: "As to your question why none of the godly discovered psychoanalysis, but only a godless Jew: Well, because piety is not the same as the genius discovering, and because the godly were for a great part not worthy to bring such an achievement to fruition. Moreover, in the first place you are not a Jew, which my boundless admiration for Amos, Isaiah, the author of Job and the prophets makes me greatly regret, and in the second place you are not so godless, since he who lives for truth lives in God and he who fights for the freeing of love 'dwelleth in God.' If you were to become aware of and experience your interpolation in the great universals which for me are as inevitable as the synthesis of the notes of a Beethoven symphony are to a musician I should say of you: There never was a better Christian."

1919 Bitter resentment arose in Austria against the Treaty of St. Germain, and the grave deterioration of the economic situation intensified the conflicts among the political parties. In the turmoil of the frontier and internal clashes, para-military organizations came into existence and continued as affiliates of the political parties in the post-war period. Despite the fact that from 1919 up to early 1934 the Social Democrats controlled the Vienna City Council, its sessions during these years were not far from anti-Jewish politics. As early as December, Monsignor Ignatz Seipel, an ascetic Catholic monk who was later to become Prime Minister, offered a resolution to pledge all parties to a program of national reconstruction on a "Christian, German, and anti-Semitic basis." In Seipel's program the Jews were to be a very useful issue through which peasant, conservative support could be consolidated.

President Wilson stated that "The Allied nations, with the fullest concurrence of our own government and people, are agreed that in Palestine shall be laid the foundations of a Jewish Commonwealth."

Sandor Ferenczi wrote Freud that he had not been receiving official recognition for his psychoanalytic accomplishments in Budapest. The Bolshevist regime in Hungary had been followed by a Roumanian occupation with strong waves of anti-Semitism. Freud wrote to him: "Keep a reserved attitude. We are not suited to any kind of official existence and we need independence in all respects. Perhaps we have reason to say: God protect us from our enemies. Moreover, there is such a thing as a future, in which we shall again find some place. We are and must remain far from tendentiousness except for the one aim of investigating and helping."

Freud was finally made full Professor at the University of Vienna. Freud called it an "empty title" since it did not allow the privilege of a seat on the Board of Faculty.

1920 By virtue of the Constitution, Vienna became federalized and enjoyed virtual autonomy. The Socialist government was led by Friedrich Adler, Otto Bauer, Karl Seitz, Julius Deutsch and Hugo Breitner.

During the years from 1881 to 1920, two million Jews entered the United States, while practically none left to return to their former countries. Seventy per cent of all these immigrants came from Russia and 25% from Austria-Hungary and Roumania.

Freud's daughter, Sophie Halberstadt died suddenly of influenzal pneumonia. He wrote to Ferenczi: "Since I am profoundly irreligious there is no one I can accuse, and I know there is nowhere to which any complaint could be expressed."

1921 Hunger riots occurred in Austria where half-starved mobs stormed markets and food shops. The relief commissioner reported that there were 400,000 homeless derelicts in Vienna alone.

Freud postulated in his *Group Psychology* the dynamism where members of the group substitute one and the same object for their ego-ideal (superego) and instead of turning the libido upon the self, deflect the energy to an association of like-minded people. They consequently identify with one another in their ego as "brothers in arms" or "brothers in Christ." Before, the infant felt he was omnipotent and his needs would be cared for as a matter of course. Now for the adult, it was the special clique who became the center and heart of creation. With excess anxiety, the organism turned for security to those who shared a similar sameness and analogous subjective awareness of life.

This individual who achieved ego identity felt that he belonged to a particular group where his past had meaning in terms of the select company's future and vice-versa. The group psychology implied a cohesive group (literally, "sticking together") where its members found membership attractive and/or purposeful and were motivated to take their roles as determined by shared understanding of their own and their group's function. In addition, they incorporated a general elevation of their own group, along with a complementary suspicion and devaluation of other groups. They found expression in the assumption that the evaluations of their own group reflected the "right" and "good" values and that those not subscribing to them were therefore often wrong and "less" good. Together, they found the greatest opportunity for satisfying individual motives. For Freud it was understandable why the Jew might prefer to be with those with whom he could feel more at ease. The Jew could take for granted certain things about his co-religionists, just as they could take for granted certain things about him.

1922 The League of Nations floated a loan of 27 million pounds and appointed a commission to supervise Austrian finances. Although the economic situation became slightly improved, the value of the *krone* (monetary unit) was destroyed.

In April, Adolf Hitler declared that the German Jews desired the defeat of their own country in World War I.

Jointly the Jewish Historical Society and the University of London sponsored a series of lectures on five Jewish philosophers: Philo, Maimonides, Spinoza, Einstein, and Freud. Freud was especially impressed with the lecture given by Israel Levine concerning the Founder of Psychoanalysis.

1923 Freud began to suffer from carcinoma and had his first serious surgical operation on his jaw. Jones told Freud of the story of a surgeon who said that if he ever arrived before the Eternal Throne, he would bring a cancerous bone and ask the Almighty why He had failed in His creative power. Freud's reply: "If I were to find myself in a similar situation, my chief reproach to the Almighty would be that He had not given me a better brain."

An abortive attempt was made by some Austrians to enter into union with Germany. More than 20,000 zealous marchers joined in the anti-Semitic parades that followed. The Rector of the Agricultural College of Austria called for an unremitting war "on the moral and economic harm brought about through the growth of Judaism and Jewish influence."

In the book *The Ego and the Id,* Freud asserted that the ego-ideal is a substitute for the early cravings for a loved father and thus contains the nucleus upon which all religions are constituted. Another study by Freud, *A Neurosis of Demonical Possession in the Seventeenth Century,* declared that originally the Devil and

God were one, but later they were divided into two opposing personalities.

A young Jew named Leyens was an avid German nationalist and a supporter of Hans Blüher. Leyens asked Freud's counsel concerning the fact that Blüher was a rabid nationalist and an anti-Semite but strangely enough also an admirer of Freud's theories. In his reply, Freud wrote some uncomplimentary remarks about Blüher but added: "I would advise you against wasting your energies in the fruitless struggle against the current political movement. Mass psychoses are proof against arguments. It is just the Germans who had occasion to learn this in the World War, but they seem unable to do so. Let them alone. . . . Devote yourself to the things that can raise the Jews above all this foolishness, and do not take amiss my advice which is the product of a long life. Do not be too eager to join with the Germans." Leyens did take Freud's advice and subsequently went to America. During the time of the Nazi uprisings, he expressed his gratitude to Freud for the sound advice. Freud responded: "You surely don't think I am proud at having been right? I was right as a pessimist against the enthusiasts, as an old man against a young one. I wish I had been wrong."

1924 There were more serious bank failures in Austria. In the United States, the Johnson Immigration Act restricted immigration from southern and eastern Europe.

Freud explained the meaning of the title, Honorary Citizen, that the city of Vienna had bestowed upon him. He said to Ferenczi: "It seems to be essentially a ritual performance, like blessing the Sabbath."

1925 Riots took place in Vienna on the occasion of the Zionist Congress, with agitation fomented by nationalist emissaries from Germany. A conference of rectors of universities held at Vienna endorsed the anti-Semitic students' demand that Jews not be allowed to attain any academic positions.

These events deeply affected Freud. In an article published in *La Revue Juive,* and then in *Imago,* under the caption "The Resistances Against Psychoanalysis," Freud recounted the various objections which were raised against his doctrine. He closed the essay with the following reflection: "In conclusion, the author might, in all reserve, submit the question whether his own personality as a Jew who would never conceal his Jewish origin, did not have some share in the antipathy which the world at large felt toward psychoanalysis. True, an objective of this sort has only seldom been uttered aloud; but, alas, we have grown so suspicious that we can hardly help surmising that the circumstance has not wholly failed to leave its impress. And perhaps it is not purely fortuitous that the first advocate of psychoanalysis has been a Jew. In order to be converted to it, a fair portion of self-sacrifice is necessary in shouldering the lot of isolation caused by opposition, a lot which the Jews are more familiar with than others."

In a letter to the Editor of the *Judische Pressezentrale* of Zurich (Jewish Central News Agency), Freud said: "I can say that I am as little an adherent of the Jewish religion as of any other religion, i.e., I consider them all most important as objects of scientific interest, but I do not share the emotional feeling that goes with them. On the other hand, I have always felt a strong feeling of kinship with my race and have also nurtured the same in my children. We have all adhered to the Jewish religion."

Freud wrote in his *Autobiographical Study:* "My parents were Jews and I have remained a Jew myself." Freud was forever interested in tracing his Jewish lineage as far back as possible. When he entered the university, he recalled in his book his feeling toward his Jewishness: "I found that I was expected to feel myself inferior and an alien because I was a Jew. I refused absolutely to do the first of these things. I have never been able to see why I should feel ashamed of my descent or, as people were beginning to say, of my race. I put up, without much regret, with my non-acceptance into the community."

Lord Balfour opened the Hebrew University on Mt. Scopus overlooking Jerusalem. Sickness kept Freud from being present but he sent this message for the occasion: "A University is a place in which knowledge is taught about all differences of religions and of nations. (A condition hardly realized in Freud's own University of Vienna.) Such an undertaking is a noble witness to the development to which our people has forced its way in two thousand years of unhappy fortune."

1926 Dr. Seipel, leader of the clericals, became Prime Minister and proceeded to profess his hatred of the Jews.

Freud, now 70, received congratulations from leaders all over the world. The University of Vienna did not send a letter of felicitation. Freud's B'nai B'rith Chapter in Vienna did celebrate his birthday. Freud replied that he was sorry that he was not well enough to attend the meeting but sent this message: "It happened that in 1895, I was subjected simultaneously to two powerful convergent influences. On the one hand I had obtained my first glimpses into the depths of the instinctual life of man, and had seen things calculated to sober or even to frighten me. On the other hand, the publication of my disagreeable discoveries led to the severance of the greater part of my human contacts: I felt as though I were despised and shunned by everyone. In this loneliness I was seized with a longing for a circle of chosen men of high character who would receive me in a friendly spirit in spite of my temerity. Your society was pointed out to me as the place where such men were to be found. What bound me to Judaism was, I must confess, not belief and not national pride, for I have always been an unbeliever and have been reared without religion, but not without respect for those requirements of human culture called 'ethical.' Whatever national pride I have, I endeavored to suppress, considering it disastrous and unjust, frightened and warned as I am by the example of what national pride has brought to the nations among whom we Jews live. But there were other considerations which made the attractiveness of Judaism and Jews irresistible—many obscure forces and emotions, all the more powerful the less they were to be defined in words; and also the clear consciousness of an inner identity in common with yours, or a common construction of the soul. And soon there was added to this the knowledge that only to my Jewish nature did I owe the two qualities which had been indispensable to me on my hard road. Because I was a Jew I found myself free from many prejudices which limited others in the use of their intellect, and, being a Jew, I was prepared to enter opposition and to renounce agreement with the 'compact majority.' " (Three Viennese psychoanalysts were members of B'nai B'rith: Freud, Eduard Hitschmann and Theodor Reik.)

He commented on his many birthday felicitations to Marie Bonaparte on May 10th: "The Jewish societies in Vienna and the University of Jerusalem (of which I am a trustee), in short the Jews altogether, have celebrated me like a national hero, although my service to the Jewish cause is confined to the single point that I have never denied my Jewishness. The official world—the University, Academy, Medical Association—completely ignored the occasion. Rightly, I think; it was only honest. With warmest greetings, your barely 70 year-old Freud."

1927 Social peace in Austria was undermined. Riots took place and the Palace of Justice was burned. The program of the Christian-Socialist party, published on New Year's Day, retained the typical anti-Semitic attitude, despite the fact that the Christian-Socialists sought the support of Jews.

Freud wrote a supplement to the essay on Michelangelo's Moses that he had published anonymously in 1914.

1928 Meetings at Innsbruck of the *International Institute for Biblical Research* were disrupted by anti-

Jewish riots following a series of lectures on the contributions of the Old Testament. Viennese police thwarted efforts by Austrian anti-Semites to bring ritual murder accusations against the Jews just before Passover and confiscated their huge quantity of anti-Jewish ritual murder literature.

Freud's book, *Humor,* was related to his earlier published work, *Wit and Its Relation to the Unconscious:* "Humor enabled man to bear suffering because it exaggerated the position of the super-ego!"

Someone wrote to Freud about the meaningfulness of "a religious experience" and "the folly of Freud's unbelief." This did not sway him. Freud said that he could only remain what he had been—"an infidel Jew."

In *The Future of an Illusion,* Freud made his strongest attack on religion. The illusion of which he wrote was religion. "An illusion," he said, "is not the same as an error, it is indeed not necessarily an error." The characteristic of an illusion is that it is derived from a person's wishes. As an example, he cited the illusion of a poor girl who dreamed that a prince would come and carry her away to his luxurious palace. It was merely a hope, though not necessarily impossible. When Freud applied illusion to religious doctrine he appeared to disregard the fact that an illusion was not necessarily an error. He said, "If after this survey we turn again to religious doctrines, we may reiterate that they are all illusions, they do not admit of proof, and no one can be compelled to consider them as true or to believe in them." Later in the same paragraph: "The riddles of the universe only reveal themselves slowly to our enquiry, to many questions science can as yet give no answer; but scientific work is our only way to the knowledge of external reality."

Thus, he continued the theme at age 71 that he had started at 51 in *Obsessive Acts and Religious Practices* —religion as a type of mass obsessional neurosis. He compared the ritual of the religious action of passing one's fingers through holy water to the compulsive act of touching one railing in three as one passes down the street. In the obsessional state of religion, the placating of the Evil Eye is achieved through characteristic compulsive thoughts and actions. Heaven is but a form of wish fulfillment. We believe in its existence because without such a belief, life on this earth would be altogether too bleak. Similarly God, the Father, is a projection of our own male parent, infinitely wise and benevolent if he is loved, or all-powerful if he is accepted with reservations.

As an illusion, religion is reminiscent of the childhood obsessional neuroses. "It has an infantile prototype and is really only the continuation of this. For once before, one had been in such a state of helplessness; as a little child in one's relationship to one's parents." Instead of a belief in God as a fixation of the all-protecting God figure, man should give up his childish illusion by helping himself with his own strength, reason, and skill. Freud did, however, emphasize that religion was valuable in that it tended to strengthen the power of society to enforce ethical behavior.

Violent anti-Semitic riots occurred at the University of Vienna and Jewish students were injured. Police help had to be invoked to restore order and the University of Vienna was forcibly closed.

By the end of the year, Palestine had 190,000 Jews.

In a pamphlet, Dr. Franz Joseph Weiss declared that "Austrian Jewry was being deliberately destroyed by means of a war of economic extermination, that thousands of Jewish merchants had been excluded from business or commerce and had been compelled to become peddlers, that an increasing number of newspaper advertisements for help stated 'Only Aryans are wanted,' and that many Jews were being excluded from all government offices and from the professions of teaching and medicine." When the Archbishop of Vienna endorsed the appeal to boycott Jewish merchants, the war of extermination upon the Jews was openly sanctioned by the Church.

Prefacing the Hebrew edition of a *General Introduction to Psychoanalysis,* Freud counted himself among the descendants of Moses and the prophets. In a few years he would expand upon this apparently conventional remark. Introducing a Hebrew translation of *Totem and Taboo,* he repeated his attitude toward being Jewish. Although he was not religious, he felt that he was a Jew in his deepest nature and had no inclination to change.

In his *Civilization and Its Discontents,* he continued to speak of religion in the spirit of *The Future of an Illusion:* "The deprivation of a need for religion from the child's feeling of helplessness and the longing it evokes for a father seems to me incontrovertible, especially since this feeling is not simply carried on from childhood days, but is kept alive perpetually by the fear of what the superior power of the fate will bring."

Freud summarized a correspondence with the novelist Romain Rolland who had inquired whether Freud would admit the sense of an all-embracing, indefinite consciousness, an "oceanic feeling," as a genuine variety of mystic experience. Freud answered, "No" and called Rolland's religious feeling "primitive." This sense "of belonging inseparably to the external world as a whole," said Freud, "is nothing but a survival of the primitive ego-feeling which is normal to infancy."

Freud's mother died. The event was seen through the eyes of her grandchild, Judith Bernays Heller: "My grandmother died in the fall of 1930, after several weeks of great weakness, of no particular ailment aside from old age and a worn-out body. Toward the end of summer, she grew weaker, and two weeks after her return to Vienna she fell into a coma and died peacefully. With her going, the strong and vivid bond that held the family together was broken."

Despite the anti-Semitism, Freud received the Goethe Prize awarded by the city of Frankfort and regarded as the supreme scientific and literary honor in Germany.

Freud wrote to Roback: "I had such a non-Jewish upbringing that today I am not able to read your dedication which is evidently in Hebrew letters. In recent years, I have often regretted this gap in my education."

1931 The collapse of the huge *Credit Anstalt* (Institution) brought down most of the financial institutions in Europe and America. In Austria, various financial scandals in which speculators of Jewish descent were involved turned public opinion even more sharply against the Jews. Unemployment continued to mount.

In a letter to Brill, Freud expressed his appreciation for the celebration of his 75th birthday in New York City. He added that he had recently undergone an operation which left him in a very depleted state of health, and expressed the concern that another one like it would probably end his life.

Freud wrote a preface to Reik's *Psychological Problems of Religion-Ritual* discussing the validity of the psychoanalytic approach to religion: "And now it became an irresistibly tempting task, indeed, a scientific duty, to extend the psychoanalytical methods of investigation from their original field to more distant and diverse spheres of mental interest. . . . The ceremonials and prohibitions of obsessional patients force us to conclude that they have created a private religion for themselves. Even the delusions of the paranoiac show an unwelcome external similarity and inner relationship to the systems of our philosophers. . . . One step is necessary before we reach the starting point for a psychoanalytical consideration of religious life. What is now the heritage of the individual was once, long ago, a newly-acquired possession, handed on from one generation to another. The Oedipus Complex itself must therefore have its own process of development and the study of prehistory can help us to find out something about it. If we submit the prehistoric and ethnological material relating to this archaic heritage to psychoanalytical elaboration, we come to an unexpectedly definite conclusion—namely, that God the father at one time walked incarnate on the earth and exercised his sovereignty as leader of the hordes of primitive men until his sons combined together and slew him. Further, the first social ties, the basic moral restrictions and the oldest form of religion—totemism—originated as a result of, and a reaction against, this liberating misdeed."

1932 A special 20 year loan of 42 million pounds sponsored by the League of Nations could not check the inflation in Austria. Various political groups fought for supremacy, the strongest being the Christian-Socialists and Social Democrats. Opposed was the Nazi Party which, following its German model, had been carefully building its propaganda machine all through the nineteen twenties. Deflation and poverty served as the stimulus to bring the Nazi membership from an inconsequential 300 to 40,000 and to supplant the old Pan-German parties with 15 seats in the Diet. During this year, the public prosecutor of Vienna confiscated several hundred thousand copies of a leaflet urging an anti-Jewish boycott. Nevertheless, anti-Jewish placards were still posted in many parts of Vienna. Early in May, representatives of Jewish organizations met in Vienna to devise means of combating increasing anti-Jewish agitation.

It was at this time that Freud concentrated even more on Jewish themes. Anti-Semitism, which pursued him all his life, became an even more pre-eminent problem. With the increase of animosity against his people, he sought to discover why he was so hated.

The response to anti-Semitism by many Jews at that time took various forms. In Nazi Germany, synagogues became crowded with worshippers. The *Hechalutz,* pioneering movement to Palestine, brought many thousands of young Jews, who had strayed from the fold, back to their homeland and in some cases back to their faith.

1933 Long before such ideas were commonplace Freud warned that the Communist approach as he saw it in Russia was doomed to disaster. In his *New Introductory Lectures on Psychoanalysis,* he said that he was convinced that the Communist promise was essentially the same as the religious promise. It was rooted in the same magical hopes and irrational fears that originated in the childhood relationship with the father. Redistribution of the world's material goods would not in itself usher in the Utopia. Freud also discussed the question of whether religious beliefs were the legitimate source of psychological investigation: "The final judgment of science on the religious *Weltanschauung* (philosophy of life) then, runs as follows. While the different religions wrangle with one another about which of them is in possession of the truth, in our view the truth of religion may be altogether disregarded. Religion is an attempt to get control over the sensory world, in which we are placed, by means of the wish-world, which we have developed within as a result of biological and psychological necessities. But it cannot achieve its end. Its doctrines carry with them the stamp of the times in which they originated, the ignorant childhood days of the human race. Its consolations deserve no trust. Experience teaches us that the world is not a nursery. The ethical commands, to which religion seeks to lend its weight, require some other foundation instead, since human society cannot do without them, and it is dangerous to link up obedience to them with religious belief. If one attempts to assign to religion its place in man's evolution, it seems not so much to be a lasting acquisition as a parallel to the neurosis which the civilized individual must pass through on his way from childhood to maturity."

In his essay *A Philosophy of Life,* he maintained that in relation to the external world, man is still a child and cannot give up the protections he enjoyed as a child. Man's belief in God has a twofold origin in the emotional strength of the memory image of the father exalted into a deity and his lasting need for protection.

But for Freud there was a more imminent danger. Hitler came to power in Germany on January 20th. Immediately he asked for wars of extermination against all Jews, even including Christians descended from Jewish parents or three Jewish grandparents.

Concurrently the Nazi Party in Austria increased considerably by the immigration of German Nazis into Austria. These imported Nazis attempted to seize political control of Austria and annex it to Germany, but Chancellor Engelbert Dollfuss resisted these efforts. A coalition of Christian-Socialists and Social Democrats might have coped with the threatening National Socialism, but the two parties were bitter enemies. The Nazi group was more than just a political party in Austria. It had all the attributes of a fanatical creed endowed with a fervor which had not been seen in Europe since the wars of religion.

It is important to note the zealous attraction to a political party with its own deification of heroes and special moral systems in a largely agnostic age.

Anti-Jewish boycott and governmental discriminations against appointments of Jews to the civil service continued. Nazism's steady march brought virtual elimination of Jews from the university life with few Jewish professors left in any faculty. An edict was promulgated forbidding Jews to practice medicine in Austrian hospitals.

In May, the Nazis burned Freud's books in Berlin in the hope that they would destroy the ideas set forth in what they called his "pornographic Jewish specialty." With the order that Jews not be permitted to serve on any scientific council, Freud finally recommended that the Christian, Boehm, replace the Jew, Max Eitingon, in order that psychoanalysis not be banned in Germany. In November, Nazi authorities demanded that the remaining German Society withdraw from membership in the International Psychoanalytical Association "because of the large number of dangerous Jews in the various international societies."

Freud still hoped that the tide would change "for us Jews." He wrote: "And as for Austria joining Germany, in which case the Jews would lose all their rights, France and her Allies would never allow that. Furthermore, Austria is not given to German brutality. In such ways we buoy ourselves up in relative security. I am in any event determined not to move from the spot." He wrote to Ferenczi: "There is no personal danger for me, and when you picture life with the suppression of us Jews as extremely unpleasant do not forget what an uncomfortable life settling abroad, whether in Switzerland or England, promises for refugees. In my opinion flight would only be justified by direct danger to life; besides, if they were to slay, one is simply one kind of death like another." (He equated physical death with exile.)

During the years 1933–1936, the figure of Moses came to the forefront of Freud's mind. Why? Said his biographer and friend, Jones: "I do not find this question hard to answer. The reason that just then narrowed Freud's interest in mankind in general and its religions to the more specific question of the Jews and their religion, could only have been the unparalleled persecution of his people that was getting under way in Nazi Germany, with the likelihood of this spreading to his native country. Like so many other Jews of that time who simply wished to live at peace with their fellow men without parading any of their particular differences from them, Freud was once more forced to wonder what it was in his people that evoked such horrible reactions, and how they had become what they were."

Newspapers reported from time to time that Freud was seriously ill and on two occasions stated that he had died. Following one of these reports, he wrote: "That the press should be so very impatient to report my obituary is surely not pleasant and must be denied on each occasion. Yet, some day it will be true and that will not be so far off. Don't you think that 77–78 years is enough for a person, especially when he can no longer do what he likes and can enjoy so little? That would be something that one could wish me for the new year."

1934 The Rome protocols of March 17th created a new relationship between Italy, Austria and Hungary. Two months later the Austrian constitution established a fascist-corporate state on Christian principles. Chancellor Dollfuss was shot to death by Nazi stormtroopers in Vienna and Kurt von Schuschnigg became his successor. Despite his pledge to the Jews of Austria that they would not be discriminated against in any way, the government did take steps to segregate Jewish children in government schools. In November, a new trade law authorized the state's economic corporations (from which Jews were barred) with the sole power to issue certificates to those in commercial undertakings. Of the 5,000 teachers in the elementary schools in Vienna, only 12 Jews could be counted by the end of the year.

Psychoanalysis was liquidated in Germany as the remaining Jewish analysts fled from the country during this year. It caused Freud much distress and confirmed his pessimistic views about the magnitude of anti-Semitism.

A Professor of Crane Theological School (Tufts) expressed his esteem for Freud's work and sent him a reprint of an article on the Emmanuel Movement. This religious group that started in Boston had the cooperation of several leading physicians in the therapeutic approach of mental treatment coupled with the reading of Scripture and prayers. Freud replied: "Perhaps one may express regret that so much energy has been expended in America in these religious movements. But America is over-rich in energy."

In August, Freud began writing *Moses and Monotheism* during the period when the shadow of Hitler loomed over all of Austria.

1935 A social insurance reform was adopted barring Jewish physicians from medical committees. The government announced that it would appoint the officers of the Vienna Bar Association and then proceeded to remove the Jewish president and members of the Board of Directors. Anti-Jewish agitation increased with the participation of Catholic lay and clerical leaders. Many voiced repeated demands for the social and economic ostracism of Jews and the introduction of a quota for converted Jews in the civil service and the professions. Intensified anti-Jewish agitation was even more pronounced by the exposure of irregularities in the management of the Austrian Phoenix Insurance Company, a few of whose officers were Jews.

The Jewish community continued to meet the successive disasters in diverse ways. In the 15 months that followed Hitler's accession to power in Germany, 4,500 Jews converted to the Catholic Church, apparently hoping that the change of religion might save them from the assaults of the rabid anti-Semites. Many applied for certificates to migrate to Palestine; indeed in two or three years the applications from Austria rose tenfold. By the end of the year, Palestine had 375,000 Jews with the larger mass of them from Eastern Europe. However, the majority of the population, members of the middle class and the proletariat, kept hoping that Nazism would be destroyed, and that some benevolent monarchy under Prince Otto would supplant it. Dreams—all dreams—of Jews who turned Catholic, of Zionists who waited for immigration certificates, of merchants who pinned their hopes on Prince Otto, of young people who put their faith in a Socialist Utopia.

All members of the German Society for Psychotherapy were expected to make a comprehensive study of Hitler's *Mein Kampf* which was now the new bible of Aryan psychoanalysis. Ernst Kretschmer immediately resigned to be replaced by Freud's former disciple, C. G. Jung. Jung's primary function was to differentiate between Aryan and Jewish psychology and to emphasize the value of the former. He edited the official organ, *Zentralblatt für Psychotherapie* (Abstracts of Psychotherapy), and editorialized how Freud and Adler had established negative psychologies because as Jews they could see only faults and not virtues. Because Jung called Freud's psychology "Jewish," a number of Freud's friends took strong exception to this statement. As one Christian expressed it, "To speak of Freud's work as 'Jewish psychology' is crypto-anti-Semitic. One may as well speak of a Jewish physics, a Jewish mathematics, or a Jewish chemistry, expressions which are indefensible in science."

Jung, after asserting the negative foundations of Jewish psychology, contrasted it with the Aryan superiority: "On the other hand, the Aryan unconscious contains tensions and creative genius and has to live up to the task of its future. . . . The Aryan unconscious has a higher potential than the Jewish and this is the advantage and also the disadvantage of a young people close to barbarism. The Jewish psychology cannot understand this and considered it nonsensical. I warned the world of this and was therefore called an anti-Semite. Freud is responsible for this. He and his Germanic followers could not understand the German psyche. They have been taught a bitter lesson by the powerful National Socialism at which the whole world looks with astonishment—a movement which pervades a whole people and is manifest in every German individual.''

Several of Freud's conversations with Joseph Wortis are worthy of mention.

January 17th

"I (Wortis) was reading a volume of Einstein's in the waiting room when Freud came in.

" 'Einstein is an interesting and likeable man,' I said, 'but his attitude toward the Jewish question is somewhat puzzling to me, and I confess I am not easily in sympathy with his or your Jewish nationalism. I wish I could clear up the problem for myself. I have no strong Jewish feelings, and up to recently was satisfied to think of myself as an American. How far ought I to let my allegiance to the Jews bring me?'

" 'That is not a problem for Jews,' said Freud, 'because the Gentiles make it unnecessary to decide; as long as Jews are not admitted into Gentile circles, they have no choice but to band together.'

" 'But how about the program for the future? I would like to see the Jews become assimilated and disappear, and Einstein talks as if they ought to be preserved forever.'

" 'The future will show how far that is possible,' said Freud. 'I personally do not see anything wrong in mixed marriages, if both parties are suited to each other. Though I must say that the chances for success seem greater in a Jewish marriage: family life is closer and warmer, and devotion is much more common. My married children have all married Jews, though it may be that they would have married Christians if they had found the right ones. It simply happens that the Gentiles who courted them or with whom they came in contact were not up to standard, and the Jews of their circle seemed superior. It may well be however that they simply did not have access to the best Christian circles. There is no reason why Jews ought not be to be perfectly friendly with Gentiles; there is no real clash of interests. But a Jew ought not to get himself baptized and attempt to turn Christian because it is essentially dishonest, and the Christian religion is every bit as bad as the Jewish. Jew and Christian ought to meet on the common ground of irreligion and humanity. Jews who are ashamed of their Jewishness have simply reacted to the mass suggestion of their society.'

" 'But I don't know what the Jews stand for,' I said. 'I can pledge allegiance to a scientific group, or a political or cultural group because they represent certain ideals, but what does Judaism stand for; in what way do its ideals differ from other group ideals?'

" 'Ruthless egotism is much more common among Gentiles than among Jews,' said Freud, 'and Jewish family life and intellectual life are on a higher plane.'

" 'You seem to think the Jews are a superior people, then,' I said.

" 'I think nowadays they are,' said Freud. 'When one thinks that ten or twelve per cent of the Nobel Prize winners are Jews and when one thinks of their other great achievements in sciences and in the arts, one has every reason to think them superior.'

" 'Jews have bad manners,' I said, 'especially in New York.'

" 'That is true,' said Freud; 'they are not always adapted to social life. Before they enjoyed emancipation in 1818 they were not a social problem, they kept to themselves—with a low standard of life it is true—but they did not go out in mixed society. Since then they have had much to learn. In countries where they have enjoyed real freedom, however, as in Italy, they are indistinguishable in this respect from Italians. The old saying is true: "Every country has the Jews that it deserves." America certainly hasn't encouraged the best kind of social conduct.'

" 'It is also said that Jews are physically inferior,' I said.

" 'That is no longer true either,' said Freud. 'Now that the Jews have access to outdoor life and the sports, you find them the equal of the Gentiles in every respect, and we have plenty of champions in all fields.' (Jones later recalled a conversation dealing with the nature of the Greek supremacy in intellectual and physical achievements to which Freud replied: "Yes, that combination is certainly preferable. For various reasons the Jews have undergone a one-sided development and admire brains more than bodies, but if I had to choose between the two I should also put the intellect first.'')

" 'And finally,' I (Wortis) said, 'the Jews are over-intellectualized; it was Jung who said, for example, that psychoanalysis bears the mark of this Jewish over-intellectualization.'

" 'So much the better for psychoanalysis then!' said Freud. " 'Certainly the Jews have a strong tendency to rationalize—that is a very good thing. What Jung contributed to psychoanalysis was mysticism, which we can well dispense with. . . . But I do not want to go too much in the direction of nationalism either,' Freud continued. 'I am not much of a Zionist—at least not the way Einstein is, even though I am one of the curators of the Hebrew University in Palestine. I recognized the great emotional force, though, of a Jewish center in the world, and thought it would be a rallying point for Jewish ideals. If it had been in the Uganda, it would not have been anything near so good. The sentimental value of Palestine was very great. Jews picture their old compatriots wailing and praying as in the olden days at the old wall—which by the way was built by Herod, not by Solomon—and felt a revival of their old spirit. I was afraid for a while though that Zionism would become the occasion for a revival of the old religion, but I have been assured by people who have been there that all the young Jews are irreligious, which is a good thing. . . . But all this,' said Freud, 'is not a psychoanalysis. However, it is worth discussing because I see you have a sincere interest in the problem. Besides it has its psychoanalytic value too: people are after all nothing but children; they believe their parents more than anybody else. If one takes a parental attitude, it is all to the good. People tend to believe those people whom they love or like. It ought not to be so, but it is.' "

January 24th

Wortis didn't like the idea of these group diagnoses, and said it makes it hard for a person to feel that he is in a marked group; it multiples his conflicts. The Jews for example are more liable to neuroses because they are looked upon as inferior.

" 'I am not so sure of that,' said Freud. 'Gentiles have plenty of neuroses too. Only the Jew is more sensitive, more critical of himself, more dependent on the judgment of others. He has less self-confidence than the Gentiles, and is fresher—has more "chootzpa" (effrontery) too—both come from the same thing. Jews are less sadistic than Gentiles, and the neuroses in general develop themselves at the cost of sadism: the more reckless a person is, the less neurotic. Besides, the Gentiles drown their neuroses in alcohol, and the Jew does not drink.'

"Anyway, it was all disturbing and confusing, I concluded, and one wished that one could work without being bothered and distracted by personalties.

" 'I am sick of fighting,' I said, 'and I don't know why we have so much of it.'

" 'For cultural reasons,' said Freud.

" 'If I were left alone,' I said, 'I would be the most harmless of animals.'

" 'And do you think you are the only one?' asked Freud."

In Berlin, a story was circulated that Jews were carrying around banners that read: "Throw us out!" Said Jones: "Naturally it was nothing but one of those savage jokes Jews seem to like making about themselves. But Freud believed it was true and wrote a bitter letter about it to Arnold Zweig in which he said he had never heard anything so revolting, and the lack of dignity it displayed was a characteristic feature of the Jews. The only consolation he could find was that the people in question were half German. His indignation at any possible self-abasement on the part of Jews reminds one of his early reaction to his father's story about picking up his cap from the gutter."

1936 An agreement was concluded between the Austrian and German governments that aimed at an amelioration of the conflict between the two states. This afforded the propaganda of the Austrian Nazis new opportunities, for Chancellor Schuschnigg felt compelled to recognize that Austria, racially and culturally, was "a German country." After the treaty, the attack upon Jewish life was broadened to include their right of citizenship and their fitness to live in the country. The campaign was no longer perpetrated by the Nazis and other extremists alone but was endorsed by the Catholic leadership as well, such as their influential monthly *Schoenere Zukunft* (Brighter Future). Nearly 60,000 of the 176,000 Viennese Jews were now registered in the welfare department as applicants for relief.

In May, Freud celebrated his 80th birthday and in

September, his Golden Wedding Anniversary. His cup of joy was diminished by the recurrence of cancer and the events which surrounded his people. Dr. M. H. Göring, a cousin of the Deputy Führer, was made the new president of the General German Medical Society for Psychotherapy with the avowed purpose of indoctrinating psychiatry with Nazi aims. Freud continued to refuse offers of foreign havens, for he would stay with his people. By this he did not mean the Austrian people. For what constituted a Jew he said is "that miraculous thing in common which—inaccessible to any analysis so far—makes the Jew." Freud would not change. He would not run. He waited and worked. He continued his writing of *Moses and Monotheism.*

Riots in Palestine compelled suspension of normal immigration.

1937 The economic condition and the political status of the Jews of Austria grew even worse as the problem of the Jewish unemployed in Vienna became graver. Not only were Jewish physicians forbidden since 1933 from practicing in Austrian hospitals, but as a result of the July decree of the Minister of Justice and Social Welfare, the Jewish doctors could no longer even practice privately. The fulfillment of the entire Nazi program—the dismissal of Jewish employees, the elimination of Jewish influence in education, the theatre, the press, the arts, and the sciences—was now achieved.

Boehm came once more to Vienna and reported for three hours on the German situation to Sigmund, Anna, and Martin Freud, Paul Federn and Jeanne

Lampl-de Groot. Sigmund's patience suddenly gave out. He broke into the exposition with the words: "Quite enough! The Jews have suffered for their convictions for centuries. Now the time has come for our Christian colleagues to suffer in their turn for theirs. I attach no importance to my name being mentioned in Germany as long as my work is presented correctly there." So saying, he left the room.

Moses and Monotheism was being written but Freud chose to withhold its publication in order to avoid adverse repercussions in Catholic countries until "the book might venture into the light of day." He deemed England, where he settled following the annexation of Austria, the country affording such "light of day."

Alfred Adler died suddenly during a lecture-tour in Aberdeen, Scotland. Adler was a Jew who spent much of his early life in Vienna, where he had joined Freud's seminar. However, in 1911 he broke with the master, for Adler rejected the views of orthodox psychoanalytic doctrine concerning the sexual origin of neurosis and contended in his School of Individual Psychology that feelings of inferiority were the true cause. He believed that a person's development was conditioned by his social environment and insisted that an individual could be analyzed and understood in terms of his present purposes of life goals rather than by his infantile past. Freud often complained that his disciple had betrayed him. When Freud learned of Adler's death, he said to a colleague who was very much moved at the news: "I don't understand your sympathy for Adler. For a Jew boy out of a Viennese suburb, a death in Aberdeen is an unheard-of career in itself and a proof of how far he got on. The world really rewarded him richly for his service in having contradicted psychoanalysis."

1938 In February, Hitler invited Schuschnigg to Berchtesgaden and persuaded him to accept two pro-Nazis as cabinet ministers. These two men, Arthur Seyss-Inquart and Edmund Glaise-Horstenau, were to undermine the authority of the Chancellor. Schuschnigg as a last resort decided to have a plebiscite on the Anschluss question, but a vote never took place because of the rioting stimulated by the Nazi elements. After two days, Schuschnigg received a phone call from Germany. Hitler ordered him to cancel the plebiscite, resign as Chancellor, and turn the administration of the country over to the Nazis or else there would be an immediate invasion. Schuschnigg was given an hour to decide the fate of a whole nation as Nazi planes zoomed overhead dropping pamphlets proclaiming: "Nazi Germany welcomes Nazi Austria." Schuschnigg tried frantically to reach Chamberlain of England, but in vain. He went to the microphone to announce his resignation and concluded with the fervent prayer: "We yield to force . . . God protect Austria." As he concluded the last word, he was arrested and taken into custody. Nazi regiments poured in from every frontier. Hitler himself followed from the market place of Linz to proclaim the unification of Austria and Germany. It was a bloodless conquest as Hitler's armies invaded and occupied the city, making Vienna the second largest city of the Third Reich and the provincial capital of the new Eastmark. Hermann Göring exalted over the conquest and invoked Deity by saying: "God did not let the Führer come into the world for nothing. He had a high mission. It is now fulfilled."

For the Jews, it was the most disastrous chapter in their long history. Tragic as was the lot of the Jews of the old Reich, the catastrophe in the protectorate of Austria was even greater. German Jews had five years to acclimate themselves to their altered circumstances and many had been able to leave their homeland. Austrian Jews, however, were suddenly plunged into a traumatic situation which they had hoped could be avoided. In Austria, there was an immediate surrender to National-Socialist "justice." Jewish men and women were seized in the streets and taken to prison without any charge being preferred. Many were taken to concentration camps and never seen again.

Austrian Nazis broke loose and avenged themselves with vicious cruelty. For weeks the Jewish inhabitants of Vienna—apart from those who had been immediately killed and arrested—were beaten and robbed. In Hitler's birthplace, degradation and pauperization of the Jews were not enough. In his first speech at Vienna, Marshal Göring proclaimed that the city must be *Judenrein,* completely cleansed of Jews. "The Jew must know we do not care to live with him. He must go." Overnight the Jews had become the plaything of the vicious mob.

Martin Freud wrote: "I have a copy of the secret instructions issued by the Vienna criminal police at this time regarding the treatment of Jews. Influential well-to-do male Jews should be arrested, provided they were not too old and gave the impression of being healthy. Their property might be destroyed without interference from the ordinary police, but if it became necessary to use fire in the destruction, care should be taken that no general conflagration was started."

Emigration from Austria was even more difficult than from Germany. All borders were barred. Suicides rose by leaps and bounds. One neutral diplomat told the *New York Times* correspondent: "I no longer try to prevent Jews from committing suicide because there is absolutely no hope for them. They come here and talk about doing it tomorrow or next week as calmly as if they were saying that they were going to make up their accounts. And what can I say?"

In the academic and cultural community, a Nazi was placed at the head of the University of Vienna. Summarily, the last few Jews were ousted from all teaching posts, including Dr. Otto Loewi of Graz University, a Nobel Prize winner in medicine. Violinist Bronislaw Huberman was scoffed at as "the Polish music Jew who violated Vienna art for years." Bruno Walter, the conductor, barely had time to escape, but his daughter was arrested. The non-Jew, Arturo Toscanini, was strangely called "King of the Jewish *mishpoche*" (family). After March 15th, not a single Jew or part-Jew remained employed in the university, the theatre, the opera, or the general press of the country.

When his books were burned in Nazi Germany, Freud made the wry observation, "What progress we are making; in the Middle Ages they would have burned me; nowadays they are content with burning my books." Now, five years later, the Nazis wanted more than his books; his life was in danger. The father of psychoanalysis, Dr. Sigmund Freud, now 82, was under house arrest. He was just another link in the chain of the academic purge. His son, Martin, said: "I think our last sad weeks in Vienna from 11th March until the end of May would have been quite unbearable without the presence of the Princess." For it was Marie Bonaparte who paid the Nazis a large ransom for Freud's life.

Ernest Jones, one of the few non-Jews in the psychoanalytic movement, related the amusing tale that when the Nazis entered Vienna, they decreed that only an "Aryan could be allowed to conduct the Psychoanalytical Clinic. Unfortunately, the only member of the Vienna Society answering to this description had just fled over the mountains to Italy. On hearing this I (Jones) cried out *'O weh; unser einziger Sabbat-Goy ist fort,'* a remark that dispelled for a moment the gloom of the gathering." (The *Sabbat-Goy* is the non-Jew who is paid to perform those chores forbidden to the traditional Jew on his Sabbath, such as kindling the fire. It means: O my God—the only Sabbath-Goy is already gone.) Jones was also unacceptable to the new regime since he had married a Jewess, the sister of Hanns Sachs.

At the last meeting of the Board of the Vienna Society it was decided that everyone should leave Austria and establish new headquarters in the country where Freud would settle. Freud commented: "After the destruction of the Temple in Jerusalem by Titus, Rabbi Jochanan ben Sakkai asked for permission to open a school at Jabneh for the study of the Torah. We are going to do the same. We are, after all, used to persecution by our history, tradition, and some of us by personal experience.'' (At the time of the destruction of Jerusalem, Jochanan ben Sakkai, a member of the Sanhedrin, had fled from the city and established a small community of sages at Jabneh, between Jaffa and Ashdod. Vespasian granted the request of ben Sakkai to found an academy there, and from that time on, Jabneh became the center of a new Jewish spiritual life.)

At literally the last possible moment, Freud escaped from the city after its capture by the Nazis. He once explained his own dream that he ''was envying some relatives who, many years earlier, had had an opportunity of removing their children to another country.'' Now his turn had come. He had to leave. Yet, he never really felt at home in Vienna where he had lived for 42 years in the same house on the same street in the same Jewish section.

When the exit permit seemed imminent he wrote to his son, Ernest, in London: ''In these dark days there are two prospects to cheer us: to rejoin you all—and—to die in freedom. I sometimes compare myself with the old Jacob whom in his old age—his children brought to Egypt. . . . It is time for *Ahasverus* (the wandering Jew) to come to rest somewhere.''

In June, the journey to London was completed. *The British Medical Journal* said: ''The medical profession of Great Britain will feel proud that their country has offered an asylum to Professor Freud and that he has chosen it as his new home.''

His first publication after leaving Austria was an article *On Anti-Semitism* which appeared in a refugee paper edited in Paris. With bitter irony Freud dug into those who deeply disliked the Jews but felt forced to protest Nazi crimes because of so-called religious or humanitarian idealism. Jews had no need of such forced tolerance. The Jews were not inferior as their devotion to spiritual and intellectual life testified.

On his arrival in London, the Yiddish Scientific Institute (YIVO) asked if they might pay their respects. Freud answered: "I was very glad to receive your greeting. You no doubt know that I gladly and proudly acknowledge my Jewishness though my attitude toward any religion, including ours, is critically negative. As soon as I recuperate to some extent from the recent events in Vienna and from tiredness after my strenuous journey I shall be glad to see you." In a letter addressed to Dr. Jacob Meitlis, Freud wrote: "So you are going to South Africa in order to revive among our people, there, interest in our scientific institute in Vilno. (The center of YIVO was Vilno, Poland.) I do not doubt that your mission will be successful. The significance of YIVO of Vilno among our other institutions you know better than I do, and you will be able to pass it on with conviction to our friends in South Africa."

While his fellow Jews in Europe were experiencing the worst persecution in their long history of suffering, the dying Freud finally completed *Moses and Monotheism* in London.

1939 The importance of the Moses theme for Freud is demonstrated in the dedication in which he devoted so much of his life to this personality. It was 38 years before, when Freud first visited Rome, that he became fascinated by Michelangelo's famous statue; and then in 1914 he published anonymously an essay about Moses in *Imago.* During the Hitler ascendancy to power in Austria, Freud began to write the first and second parts of *Moses and Monotheism* which he completed during the year of his death. Naturally, there were psychologists and religionists who found different meanings and significance in Freud's last book. Some psychoanalysts decried the attempt to determine the validity of the book's contents on the basis of Freud's hostility to organized religion. Other psychologists such as Bakan claimed: "There can be little doubt that this book, which is Freud's most intense expression of his concern with the problem of Judaism, must in some sense have been a response to the outward events of his life. To say that Freud wrote it as a reaction to his experience of the force of anti-Semitism must hit at the truth in some way." Choisy concurred: "It is Freud's deathbed confession. In it are engraved the secret hieroglyphics of the total Freud." Therefore, it is important to reconstruct Freud's *Moses* and to delve into the analyses of his psychoanalytic colleagues.

Freud set out with postulates based largely on J. H. Breasted, *History of Egypt* (1906) and *Dawn of Conscience* (1934), but the major rationale for his theories came from Ernst Sellin's *History of the Israeli-Jewish Religion* (1922). Sellin was an acknowledged anti-Semite and his original theses, which served as Freud's guiding principles, were allegedly withdrawn and repudiated by this German exegete. Noted Biblical scholar, Abraham Yahuda, finished a review of Freud's book with the words: "It seems to me that in these words we hear the voice of one of the most fanatical Christians in his hatred of Israel and not the voice of Freud who hated and despised such fanaticism with all his heart and strength."

Freud began by de-Judaizing the greatest Jew in history. He said that Moses was an Egyptian, not a Jew! The derivation of the name was Egyptian (*mose,* "child") contrary to the text of the Hebrew *mashah* (to draw from the water). Moses was slow of speech "not because he had a speech impediment but because he spoke Egyptian and needed an interpreter." In short, Moses was not a Jew.

In addition, Moses was characterized as more than just an average citizen for he was of noble origin, "an august Egyptian . . . who brought his retinue with him, his nearest adherents, his scribes, his servants." Moses received his monotheism from Amenhotep IV who reigned as Ikhnaton from 1375 to 1358, before the Christian Era. The Aton or sun-religion (*aton-adonai-adonis*) was a universal monotheistic God-faith that permitted no image worship and stressed ethical attributes. When Ikhnaton died, there arose a violent reaction of the disenfranchised pagan priests of Amon who once again reintroduced polytheism and brought the end of "the glorious eighteenth dynasty." Ikhnaton had no successor but a son-in-law who now deserted Aton. There was but one intimate follower—Moses, a man of high rank. Moses revived the Aton faith but instead of the sun-god chose *Jahve,* a volcano deity that resided in the Sinai-Horeb mountain. Moses taught the faith to the Habiri tribes of Aramaeans living in Goshen who decided to live their own lives with the God of Moses. Thus Moses the Egyptian acquired a belief in monotheism and converted the Jews to it.

Why this enormous detail to Moses? Here the psychologists have a "field day." Some say that there is a long-standing myth—a fantasy common to every child unhappy with his parents—of believing that he was a prince smuggled by chance into the household of ordinary peasants. David Bakan said, "By creating a Gentile Moses of high position and royal lineage, he overcomes his sense of the Jew as a person of low social status. Freud, as we know from various biographical items, felt very sensitive about the low social position to which his Jewishness held him. Freud's myth that the Jews were adopted by a Gentile of high nobility overcomes the sense of degradation." And another comment by Lydia Oehlschlegel: "Religio-psychoanalytical investigation discloses the fact that Freud's attempt to prove Moses an Egyptian, and the monotheistic religion, which Moses actually revived and reaffirmed to the ancient Hebrews, an Egyptian religion (thus denying the Jewishness of both), was prompted by his repressed resentment of his own Jewishness, a resentment that was aroused by the realization that being a Jew kept him powerless to obtain redress for the diverse injustices to which his people were often subjected by ill-bred Gentiles. The realization that being a Jew made him, 'the strong man,' helpless in the face of humiliation and oppression was almost more than he could bear, and it was doubtlessly that feeling of helplessness before a widespread wrong which aroused in him the wish to be a Gentile, because only as such could he hope to secure a position of sufficient power and influence to enable him to fight for truth and justice without restraint."

According to Freud, Moses introduced circumcision, a specifically Egyptian rite, to the Israelites. He continued: "The fact remains that the question concerning the origin of circumcision has only one answer; it comes from Egypt." Freud's purpose in dwelling on this point was two-fold. He wanted to reinforce the theory of Part I "Moses, *an Egyptian*"; secondly, by attributing circumcision to the Egyptians, he hoped to lessen the prevalent anti-Semitism. He said: "The deeper motives of anti-Semitism have their roots in times long past; they come from the unconscious, and I am quite prepared to hear that what I am going to say will at first appear incredible. I venture to assert that the jealousy which the Jews evoked in other peoples by maintaining that they were the first-born, favorite child of God the Father, has not yet been overcome by those others, just as if the latter had given credence to the assumption." Freud transposed the noxious and hurtful characteristics of circumcision and "chosen people" concepts to non-Jewish origins.

Freud continued by stating that circumcision was that borrowed tradition which had already caused the Jew too much anguish: "Among the customs through which the Jews marked off their aloof position, that of circumcision made a disagreeable, uncanny impression on others." Envy plays an important role in anti-Semitism. The same is true of the "chosen people concept" where the Jew reputedly believed himself superior to all other peoples. Then the thesis is counterposed that the Jews were not God's chosen people but rather the chosen people of Moses. In Freud's words: "Sometimes, it is true, we hear of a people adopting another god, but never of a god choosing a new people. Perhaps we approach an understanding of this unique happening when we reflect on the connection between Moses and the Jewish people. Moses had stooped to the Jews, had made them his people; they were his 'chosen people.' "

Still another supposition of Freud is that the Egyptian leader was killed by the Jews who acted out again the killing of the primal father portrayed in *Totem and Taboo*. Because of a lasting unconscious sense of guilt, the Jews became monotheistic attempting to repent for their crime against the ancient father by magnifying him above all else. In commenting on this hypothesis, Bakan proclaims that Freud had projected a current fantasy on to a past situation, which is what is done in all mythmaking: "It is Freud who wishes that Moses were murdered; and by this, of course, he must mean he wishes that the current repressive and oppressive force associated with the Mosaic image would be killed. What Jacob Frank did literally when he cut up the Torah to make shoes of the parchment for his friends, Freud does in his own way through myth. And Jacob Frank's assertion that the Torah was dead, Freud repeats with psychoanalytic sophistication." Ernst Simon conjectured that the significance of the murder of the father is not taken to be entirely negative. "The murder of the father by his son is but a subtle and dialectical form of identification with him."

Still another, A. A. Brill, saw in this fantasy a theme which hearkened back to one Freud had introduced in *Totem and Taboo.* "Every great leader, every teacher of a new truth or a new way of living, had to be sacrificed in order to gain the ascendancy of his ideas, just as the totem animal when it had been eaten by the worshipers was mourned and then deified after its resurrection."

These are then the highlights of Freud's *Moses and Monotheism.* There was less than an enthusiastic response even though Freud wrote to Hanns Sachs: "The *Moses* is not an unworthy leavetaking." Commented W. F. Albright: His new book is totally devoid of serious historical method and deals with historical data . . . cavalierly." T. J. Meek could see little relationship between the religious thought of the Hebrews and that of Egypt and Mesopotamia and said: "It is one of the enigmas of history that the Hebrews were so little affected by the religion of Egypt." Erich Fromm cited his own explanation of the underlying reason that provoked Freud to make Moses a distinguished Egyptian who put himself at the head of the enslaved Israelites and gave them the religion which a former enlightened Pharaoh had imposed upon his subjects. For it was Moses who embodied Freud's ego-ideal. . . . "He did something, not against Moses, but against the Jews: he deprived them not only of their hero, but also of the claim to the originality of the monotheistic idea. . . . If this had been Freud's field, or if his proof had been overwhelming, no psychological questions need be asked as to the motive of Freud's publication of *Moses and Mono-*

theism. But since this is not so, one must assume that Freud's preoccupation with Moses was rooted in the deep unconscious identification with him. Freud, like the great leader of the Jews, had led the people to the promised land without reaching it himself; he had experienced their ingratitude and scorn without giving up his mission."

Moses and Monotheism was condemned by clergymen of all denominations. This is understandable since to his dying day in his last pages of his last book, Freud proclaimed both his atheism and the conviction that religious belief was but an illusion that could only be explained psychologically: "I do not believe that one supreme great God 'exists' today, but I believe that in primeval times there was one person who did appear gigantic and who, raised to the status of a deity, was returned to the memory of men." A Jewish leader, Morris Raphael Cohen, used these words of derision: "If anyone else had written this book, we should have been justified in dismissing it as the work of an opinionated crank who is more interested in his tortuous speculation than in getting at the verifiable facts." Yet one part of the volume was complimentary, portraying a favorable description of the Jews' characteristics, notably their self-confidence, their tenacity, and their preference for intellectual pursuits. Freud suggested that the belief in a Messiah originated in the wish that the murdered Father-Moses would return. Mosaic religion had been a Father religion. Christianity became a Son religion. The old God, the Father, took second place. Christ, the Son, stood in His place, just as in those dark times every son had longed to do.

But the monotheism of the Jew demanded an exclusive bending to the Father-God. Morality could more readily ensue from the authority of the Paternal God, for Patriarchy made more vigorous demands upon the individual. The Jewish Father-God granted no rights of existence to other deities and was more strict in ethical claims.

When selections of *Moses and Monotheism* had already been published in *Imago,* important Jewish leaders pleaded with Freud not to publish the book since it would only further demoralize the Jews in their hour of greatest trial. Freud explained in the very first sentence why he had to deny the Jewish people their greatest son by making him an Egyptian. "Such a deed," he says, "is not to be undertaken lightheartedly—especially by one belonging to that people. But truth is truth." A month before he died, he was invited to replace Dr. Moses Gaster as President of the London YIVO when Freud replied: "Because of the active opposition which my book *Moses and Monotheism* evoked in Jewish circles I doubt whether it would be in the interests of YIVO to bring my name before the public eye in such a capacity. I leave the decision to you."

Shortly before midnight on September 23rd, Sigmund Freud passed away. Ernest Jones delivered the eulogy: "And so we take leave of a man whose life we shall not know again."

As to the extent of the meaning of his life and thought in the field of religion in general, and Judaism in particular, one can only quote from Freud's words: "I leave the decision to you."

EPILOGUE

Jean-Paul Sartre in his book, *Anti-Semite and the Jew,* described the Jew in an unfriendly world. The authenic Jew "knows that he is one who stands apart, untouchable, scorned, proscribed—and it is as such that he asserts his being. He stakes everything on human grandeur for he accepts the obligation to live in a situation that is defined precisely by the fact that it is unlivable; he derives his pride from his humiliation. The moment he ceases to be passive, he takes away all power and virulence from anti-Semitism." In essence, Sartre is stating that the authentic Jew, like any other authentic person, is what he makes of himself. The Jew must realize the isolation of his position, accept it, and only then can he become a whole person. Man's authenticity is rooted in freedom and responsibility. Freedom is not an abstraction to be generically applied to "man" as such, but a risk, a venture, and a demand.

This book is about the life of a man and his mode of living in freedom and responsibility. Thus, when Freud's enemies attacked his unimpeachable private life, his friends became deeply disturbed. "It seems so unfair," they said angrily. Sandor Ferenczi, especially, attempted to comfort the master: "Well, they are afraid of you now. Later on, it will calm down and they'll praise you." Freud paused and then retorted,

"I don't think so. They'll always throw stones at me. You see, I have troubled humanity's sleep."

The inner individual struggles of a man with his external environment must inevitably end. Yet, Sigmund Freud's story never ends, for his works continue to invade the inner recesses of our minds and disturb our sleep.

CREDITS AND BIBLIOGRAPHY

Abrahams, Israel. *Jewish Life in the Middle Ages.* Philadelphia: The Jewish Publication Society of America, 1896.

Ackerman, Nathan W. and Jahoda, Marie. *Anti-Semitism and Emotional Disorder, A Psychoanalytic Interpretation.* New York: Harper and Brothers, 1950.

Agus, Jacob B. *It's The Mythology.* National Jewish Monthly, pp. 20–22. September, 1964.

Albright, William F. *From the Stone Age to Christianity.* Baltimore: The Johns Hopkins Press, 1946.

Alexander, Franz. *Our Age of Unreason.* Philadelphia: Lippincott, 1942.

Anti-Semitism, Austria. The Universal Jewish Encyclopedia, Volume I, pp. 354–357. New York: Universal Jewish Encyclopedia Co., Inc., 1948.

Austria. The Jewish Encyclopedia, Volume II, pp. 321–325. New York and London: Funk and Wagnalls Company, 1909.

Bakan, David. *Moses in the Thought of Freud.* Commentary, pp. 322–331. October, 1958.

———. *Sigmund Freud and the Jewish Mystical Tradition.* Princeton: D. Van Nostrand Company, Inc., 1958.

Bell, Daniel. *Reflections on Jewish Identity.* Commentary, pp. 471–478. June, 1961.

Bettelheim, Bruno. *The Victim's Image of the Anti-Semite.* Commentary, pp. 173–179. February, 1948.

Biddle, W. Earl. *Integration of Religion and Psychiatry.* New York: Collier Books, 1962.

Binswanger, Ludwig. *Sigmund Freud: Reminiscences of a Friendship.* New York and London: Grune and Stratton, 1957.

Brill, Abraham A. *The Basic Writings of Sigmund Freud.* New York: The Modern Library, 1938.

———. *Reflections, Reminiscences of Sigmund Freud.* Magazine.

Choisy, Maryse. *Sigmund Freud: A New Appraisal.* New York: Philosophical Library, Inc., 1963.

Dempsey, Peter J. *Freud, Psychoanalysis, Catholicism.* Cork, Ireland: Mercier Press, 1956.

Deutsch, Gotthard. *Anti-Semitism.* The Jewish Encyclopedia, Volume I, pp. 641–649. New York: Funk and Wagnalls, 1909.

Dimont, Max I. *Jews, God and History.* New York: Simon and Schuster, 1962.

Dollard, John. *Caste and Class in a Southern Town.* New York: Harper, 1937.

Dubnow, Semen M. *History of the Jews in Russia and Poland.* I, II, III. Philadelphia: The Jewish Publication Society of America, 1916–1920.

Dunner, Joseph. *The Republic of Israel.* New York: McGraw-Hill Book Company, Inc., 1950.

Edinger, Dora. *Bertha Pappenheim.* The Reconstructionist, Volume XXI, pp. 22–24. March 18, 1955.

Elbogen, Ismar. *A Century of Jewish Life.* Philadelphia: The Jewish Publication Society of America, 1946.

Elliott, Robert. *The Perkins School of Theology Journal,* 14:47. Winter, 1960.

Erikson, Erik H. *Growth and Crises of the Healthy Personality.* The Healthy Personality. (ed. M. E. Senn) pp. 91–146. New York: Josiah Macy, Jr. Foundation, 1950.

Feldman, S. S. *Jung and National Socialism.* American Journal of Psychiatry. September, 1945.

Freud, Anna. *The Ego and the Mechanisms of Defence.* London: Hogarth Press, 1954.

Freud, Ernest L. *Letters of Sigmund Freud.* New York: Basic Books, Inc., 1961.

Freud, Martin. *Sigmund Freud: Man and Father.* New York: The Vanguard Press, 1958.

Freud, Sigmund. *An Autobiographical Study.* New York: W. W. Norton and Company, Inc., 1952.

———. *The Basic Writings of Sigmund Freud.* (trans. A. A. Brill) New York: Modern Library, 1938.

———. *Civilization and Its Discontents.* (trans. Joan Riviere) London: Hogarth Press, 1930.

———. *Collected Papers.* (ed. James Strachey) (5 Volumes). London: Hogarth Press, 1950–1952.

———. *The Ego and the Id.* London: Hogarth Press, 1927.

———. *The Future of an Illusion.* (trans. W. D. Robinson-Scott) London: Hogarth Press, 1928.

———. *Group Psychology and the Analysis of the Ego.* London: International Psychoanalytic Press, 1922.

———. *The Interpretation of Dreams.* (trans. and ed. James Strachey) New York: Basic Books, Inc., 1955.

———. *Leonardo da Vinci: A Psychosexual Study of an Infantile Reminiscence.* New York: Moffat, Yard and Co., 1916.

———. *The Origins of Psychoanalysis: Letters to Wilhelm Fliess, Drafts and Notes: 1887–1902.* (eds. Bonaparte, M.; Freud, A.; and Kris, E.) New York: Basic Books, Inc., 1954.

———. *Moses and Monotheism.* (trans. K. Jones) New York: Alfred A. Knopf, Inc., 1939.

———. *A Neurosis of Demonical Possession in the Seventeenth Century.* Collected Papers, IV.

———. *New Introductory Lectures on Psycho-Analysis.* (trans. W. J. H. Sprott) London: Hogarth Press, 1933.

———. *Obsessive Acts and Religious Practices.* Collected Papers, Volume II. London: Hogarth Press, 1924.

———. *On Being of the B'nai B'rith.* Commentary, pp. 23–24. March, 1946.

———. *On Narcissism.* Collected Papers, Volume IV, pp. 30–59. London: Hogarth Press, 1948.

———. *On the Psychopathology of Everyday Life.* New York: Macmillan Company, 1914.

———. *Totem and Taboo.* (trans. James Strachey) London: Routledge and Kegan Paul, 1950.

———. *Wit and Its Relation to the Unconscious.* (Introduction by A. A. Brill) New York: Moffat, Yard and Co., 1916.

Friedenwald, Harry. *The Jew and Medicine: Essays.* Baltimore: The Johns Hopkins Press, 1944.

Fromm, Erich. *Sigmund Freud's Mission.* New York: Grove Press, Inc., 1959.

Gilbert, Arthur. *The Jewish Freud and Self-Hatred.* (four pages) 515 Madison Avenue, New York, N.Y.

Glazer, Nathan. *The "Alienation" of Modern Man.* Commentary, pp. 378–385. April, 1947.

Graeber, Isacque; Britt, Stewart H.; and Britt, Miriam. *Jews in a Gentile World.* The Macmillan Company, 1942.

Graetz, Heinrich. *History of the Jews.* III, IV, V. Philadelphia: The Jewish Publication Society of America, 1945.

Graf, Max. *Reminiscences of Professor Sigmund Freud.* Psychoanalytic Quarterly II, pp. 465–476. 1942.

Grollman, Earl A. *Judaism and the Intellectual.* The Jewish Spectator, pp. 7–9. October, 1964.

———. *Some Sights and Insights of History, Psychology and Psychoanalysis Concerning the Father-God and Mother-Goddess Concepts of Judaism and Christianity.* The American Imago. Volume 20, pp. 187–209. Summer, 1963.

Guirdham, Arthur. *Christ and Freud.* New York: Collier Books, 1962.

Guthrie, Edwin R. and Edwards, Allen L. *Psychology.* New York: Harper, 1949.

Halborn, Hajo. *Austria.* The Encyclopedia Americana, Volume II, pp. 623–633. 1960.

Hall, Calvin S. *A Primer of Freudian Psychology.* New York: Mentor Books, 1963.

Heller, Judith Bernays. *Freud's Mother and Father: A Memoir.* Commentary, pp. 418–421. May, 1956.

Hyman, Stanley. *Freud and Boas: Secular Rabbis?* Commentary, pp. 264–267. March, 1954.

Jones, Ernest. *The Life and Work of Sigmund Freud.* Volumes I, II, and III. New York: Basic Books, Inc., 1953–1957.

Kagan, Henry E. *Sigmund Freud, The Jew.* Pamphlet, 1957.

———. *Six Who Changed the World.* New York: Thomas Yoseloff, Publisher, 1963.

Kaskeline, Egon. *Vienna.* The Encyclopedia Americana, Volume 28, pp. 78–81. 1960.

Kastein, Joseph. *History and Destiny of the Jews.* New York: The Viking Press, 1933.

Klausner, Samuel Z. *Psychiatry and Religion.* New York: The Free Press of Glencoe, 1964.

Klineberg, Otto. *Social Psychology.* New York: Henry Holt and Company, 1940.

Kroeber, Alfred L. *Anthropology.* New York: Harcourt, Brace, and Company, 1948.

Levinger, Elma. *The Story of the Jew.* New York: Behrman, 1945.

Levinger, Lee J. *A History of the Jews in the United States.* New York: Union of American Hebrew Congregations, 1956.

Lewin, Kurt. *Resolving Social Conflict.* New York: Harper and Brothers, 1948.

Linn, Louis and Schwarz, Leo. *Psychiatry and Religious Experience.* New York: Random House, 1958.

Malinowski, Bronislaw. *Sex and Repression in Savage Society.* London: K. Paul, Trench, Trubner, 1927.

Margolis, Max L. and Marx, Alexander. *A History of the Jewish People.* Philadelphia: The Jewish Publication Society of America, 1927.

McClelland, David C. *Religious Overtones in Psychoanalysis.* The Ministry and Mental Health. (ed. Hans Hofmann) New York: Association Press, 1960.

Mead, Margaret. *Culture and Personality.* The Encyclopedia of Mental Health, Volume II.

Meek, Theophile J. *Hebrew Origins.* New York: Harper, 1950.

Meitlis, Jacob. *The Last Days of Sigmund Freud.* Jewish Frontier, pp. 20–22. September, 1951.

Mowrer, Orval Hobart. *The Crisis in Psychiatry and Religion.* Princeton: D. Van Nostrand Company, Inc., 1961.

Mowshowitz, Simon. *Josef Samuel Bloch.* The Universal Jewish Encyclopedia, II, pp. 400–401. 1940.

Munroe, Ruth L. *Schools of Psychoanalytic Thought.* New York: Holt, Rinehart and Winston, 1955.

Myrdal, Gunnar. *An American Dilemma.* New York: Harper and Brothers, 1944.

Noveck, Simon. *Judaism and Psychiatry.* New York: National Academy for Adult Jewish Studies, 1956.

Oehlschlegel, Lydia. *Regarding Freud's Book on "Moses."* The Psychoanalytic Review, Volume XXX, 1943.

Ostow, Mortimer. *Religion.* American Handbook of Psychiatry, II. New York: Basic Books, Inc., 1959.

Parkes, James W. *An Enemy of the People: Anti-Semitism.* New York: Penguin Books, Inc., 1945.

———. *The Jewish Problem in the Modern World.* London: Oxford University Press, 1946.

Pelcovits, N. A. *What About Jewish Anti-Semitism?* Commentary, pp. 118–125. February, 1947.

Pfister, Oskar. *The Psychoanalytic Method.* New York: Moffat, Yard and Company, 1917.

Philp, Howard L. *Freud and Religious Belief.* London: Camelot Press, Ltd., 1956.

Progoff, Ira. *The Death and Rebirth of Psychology.* New York: The Julian Press, Inc., 1956.

———. *Depth Psychology and Modern Man.* New York: The Julian Press, Inc., 1959.

Puner, Helen W. *Freud: His Life and Mind.* New York: Howell, Soskin, Publishers, 1947.

Reik, Theodor. *From Thirty Years with Freud.* (trans. Richard Winston) New York, Toronto: Farrar and Rinehart, 1940.

———. *Jewish Wit.* New York: Gamut Press, 1962.

———. *Ritual.* New York: Farrar, Strauss and Company, Inc., 1946.

———. *The Search Within.* New York: Farrar, Strauss, and Cudahy, 1956.

Rieff, Philip. *Freud: The Mind of the Moralist.* New York: The Viking Press, 1959.

Roback, Abraham A. *Freudiana.* Cambridge, Massachusetts: Sci-Art Publishers, 1957.

———. *Jewish Influence in Modern Thought.* Cambridge, Massachusetts: Sci-Art Publishers, 1929.

Roheim, Géza. *Psychoanalysis and Anthropology.* Psychoanalysis Today. (ed. Sandor Lorand) London: Allen and Unwin, 1948.

Rose, Arnold. *Anti-Semitism's Root in City Hatred.* Commentary, pp. 374–378. October, 1948.

Rosenberg, Bernard and Shapiro, Gilbert. *Marginality and Jewish Humor.* Midstream, pp. 70–80. Summer, 1958.

Rubenstein, Richard L. *Psychoanalysis and the Origins of Judaism.* The Reconstructionist, pp. 11–20. December 2, 1960.

Sachar, Abram L. *A History of the Jews.* New York: Alfred A. Knopf, 1960.

———. *Sufferance is the Badge.* New York and London: Alfred A. Knopf, 1939.

Salter, Andrew. *The Case Against Psychoanalysis.* New York: The Citadel Press, 1964.

Sartre, Jean-Paul. *Anti-Semite and the Jew.* New York: Shocken Books, Inc., 1948.

———. *Portrait of the Inauthentic Jew.* Commentary, pp. 389–397. May, 1948.

Schoenwald, Richard L. *Freud: The Man and His Mind.* New York: Alfred A. Knopf, 1956.

Shirer, William L. *The Rise and Fall of the Third Reich.* New York: Simon and Schuster, 1960.

Simon, Ernst. *Sigmund Freud, the Jew.* Publications of the Leo Baeck Institute of Jews from Germany. Year Book II, pp. 270–307. London: 1957.

Steinberg, Milton. *The Making of the Modern Jew.* New York: Behrman House, 1944.

Steindletz, E. *Hasidism and Psychoanalysis.* Judaism, Volume 9, Number 3, pp. 222–228. Summer, 1960.

Strodtbeck, Fred L. *Family Interaction, Values and Achievement.* Talent and Society. Princeton: D. Van Nostrand Company, Inc., 1958.

Tocqueville, Alexander. *Democracy in America.* New York: George Dearborn, 1838.

Wechsler, L. B. *The Neurologist's Point of View.* New York: L. B. Fischer, 1945.

Weinstein, Jacob J. *Anti-Semitism.* The American Jew. (ed. Oscar Janowsky) New York and London: Harper and Brothers, 1942.

Werner, Alfred. *Joseph Popper.* Universal Jewish Encyclopedia, VIII, pp. 600–601. 1948.

Wirth, Louis. *The Ghetto.* Chicago: The University of Chicago Press, 1928.

Witner, Helen G. *Some Parallels Between Psychiatry and Cultural Anthropology.* The American Journal of Orthopsychiatry. Volume IX, pp. 95–102. Number 1, January, 1939.

Wittels, Fritz. *Sigmund Freud: His Personality, His Teachings, and His School.* New York: Dodd, Mead and Company, 1924.

Wolfenstein, Martha. *Two Types of Jewish Mothers.* Childhood in Contemporary Cultures. Chicago: University of Chicago Press, 1955.

Wortis, Joseph F. *Fragments of an Analysis with Freud.* New York: Charter Books, 1963.

Zborowski, Mark and Herzog, Elizabeth. *The Place of Book-Learning in Traditional Jewish Culture.* Childhood in Contemporary Society. Chicago: University of Chicago Press, 1955.

Zilboorg, Gregory. *Sigmund Freud: His Exploration of the Mind of Man.* New York: Scribner's Sons, Ltd., 1951.

INDEX